REDWOOD WRITING PROJECT

On Their Way

On Their Way

Celebrating Second Graders
as They Read and Write

JANE FRASER & DONNA SKOLNICK

HEINEMANN
Portsmouth, NH

Heinemann
A division of Reed Elsevier Inc.
361 Hanover Street
Portsmouth, NH 03801-3912
Offices and agents throughout the world

Excerpt from Leland Jacob's column, "The Child Writer" reprinted with permission of the publisher, Teaching K–8, Norwalk, CT 06854. From the August/September 1987 issue of *Teaching K–8*.

Acquisitions Editor: Carolyn Coman
Production Editor: Renée M. Pinard
Cover Designer: Darci Mehall

Library of Congress Cataloging-in-Publication Data

Fraser, Jane.
    On their way : celebrating second graders as they read and write / Jane Fraser and Donna Skolnick.
        p.   cm.
    Includes bibliographical references (p.   ).
    ISBN 0-435-08830-0
    1. Language arts (Elementary)—United States.   2. Reading (Elementary)—United States.   3. English language—Composition and exercises—Study and teaching (Elementary)—United States.
    4. Second grade (Education)—United States.   I. Skolnick, Donna.
    II. Title.
    LB1576.F72   1994
    372.6—dc20   94-3695
                                                                              CIP

Printed in the United States of America on acid-free paper.
99 98 97 96   EB   4 5 6

For Julius, who provides the support while lighting the way.
J.F.

For Harv, Sara, and Scott,
who take a piece of my
heart with them wherever
they go.
D.S.

Contents

Acknowledgments

We did not write this book alone. In many respects we share the thoughts and ideas with our second-grade students who taught us the excitement of learning in a community. Some of them are represented in this book either by their stories or their work. Others are there without direct recognition, resting as a subtext that supports our work and thinking. Our students taught us to seek patterns, diversity, excitement, change, and new ideals as we worked and learned together.

Some of our colleagues' names could appear many times in these acknowledgments. In our after-school teacher-research group, Caltha Crowe, Anne Nesbitt, Hilda Rhodes, Ann Shames, Claire Shumofsky, and Mary Lou Woodruff, among others, joined us in the search. Occasionally we met with a middle school group of researchers in our district led by Karen Ernst.

As staff development teachers, we learned in the classrooms of other Westport staff members. We taught, researched, planned, and debriefed together. We tried new ideas. We especially want to thank Sue Bambach, Dana Barsi, Sylvia Barton, Hallie Cirino, Caltha Crowe, JoAnn Davidson, Karen Emanuelson, Sheila Florio, Bobbi Hauer, Jacque O'Brien, Shelley Rasch, Hilda Rhodes, Ann Shames, Karen Stafford, Peter von Euler, Mary Lou Woodruff, and Wendy Wu.

Our classroom work has been enhanced by the competent staff in the Children's Services at the Westport Public Library led by Ellen Fader. Ellen strongly believes in community outreach and was a catalyst for cooperation between the library and the schools. Her knowledge of children's literature and her enthusiasm for helping teachers use literature in their classrooms were unparalleled.

The Westport schools are a unique place to work because of the quality of the staff members, who are encouraged to continue their search and their learning. We want to thank Mort Sherman, who was the assistant superintendent for curriculum when we worked in staff development. He inspired, challenged, and cajoled us, letting us fly on our own wings to new destinations. We also appreciate our administrator at the Coleytown School where we returned to the classroom to teach second grade. Dan Sullivan allowed us to be ourselves and supported our learning with good listening and questions.

Our colleagues, who shared the ups and downs of working townwide in the classrooms of other teachers, deserve special mention: Marion Bailey, Pat Beasley, Holly Church, JoAnn Davidson, Judy Hall, Betty Honeycomb, and Kaye May gave us support and empathy—and continue to do so to this day. We don't want to forget Sam Blanc and Fran Hennessey of the Teachers' Center, who helped solve our daily problems.

The idea for our cover came from Kate Sanderson, a friend and fellow teacher. Our cover artists are Tommy Haberstroh, Gabrielle Utting, Derek Anderson, and Meredith Katz.

In the 1970s we began to attend evening meetings organized by June Gould, Bena Kallick, and Joanna Nicholson. A small cadre of learners began to look at education with an eye to making positive changes in the curriculum and structure of classrooms. June, Bena, and Joanna have gone on to do their own individual work in education, and the other group members—like ourselves—have done likewise; we are all stronger for our participation in that group.

We want to thank Lucy McCormick Calkins for her inspiration and challenge. She encouraged us to write this book.

Donna wants to give a special thank-you to June Gould, the first person to ask, would you like to tell your stories? Her thanks also extend to the members of that writing group: Holly Church, Judy Luster, Jim Wheeler, and Mary Winsky. What joyful memories! She also thanks her family of incredible teachers and learners, which includes Esther Frederickson, Nancy Fellows, Karen Fitzgerald, Suzanne van Valkenberg, and Betty Jones.

For twelve years Jane has enjoyed observing her grandchildren acquire and use language before they moved on to become avid readers and writers themselves. She road tested many books with them and found new resources in the books selected by their parents. She also thanks the other writer in the family, her husband.

Our second-grade colleague Anne Nesbitt deserves special mention. Her influence underlies much of what we have written here. Our daily lunches were filled with intense personal and philosophical conversations that digressed into new meanings. We thank you, Anne, for your insights, your humor, and your gentle intelligence.

A final thank-you goes to Carolyn Coman and Renée Pinard, our supportive editors at Heinemann. Their commitment to our manuscript helped ease the way and made this project a pleasure.

Introduction

Imagine Jordan, age seven, so engrossed in *Herbie Jones and the Dark Attic* (Kline 1992) that he does not know the class is in line for gym. Picture Gabrielle, finishing a project on hermit crabs that has taken her three weeks to complete, or David, who talks with his father about authors and cannot believe his father is not familiar with the work of William Steig or Bill Peet. For us, watching second graders become habitual readers and writers is like taking a long drink at a cool spring. Their enthusiasm and commitment as they read and write convinced us to share our vision and practice.

Eight years ago we worked as reading and writing staff development teachers in kindergarten-through-grade-six classrooms throughout our school district. Our jobs were rotational; we knew we would return to the classroom. We talked often about what grade level we preferred. We had both taught fourth grade and Jane had had a long stint as a first-grade teacher.

We agreed on one thing: second grade was not high on our list. That year seemed suspended between the excitement of learning to read and the academic challenges and enthusiasm of later grades. We witnessed several classrooms where second grade had become a final resting place for teachers who wanted to have a peaceful day. Or at least, that's what we thought then.

By a stroke of luck, we both ended up in the same school and teaching second grade. The major surprise was that we couldn't have been more mistaken about working with seven- and eight-year-olds.

We made three important discoveries. Much had changed in elementary education and in our own thinking, and we had underestimated the marvelous potential and energy of these young learners.

Second grade is a dynamic year of growth and minimiracles. It is *not* a quiet year of consolidation and transition sandwiched between the first and third grades. We might even argue that it eclipses the other primary grades for fun and adventure since second-grade classes are not caught up in the constraints and pressures of the first grade and learning to read. Nor are second-grade classes bound by all the curriculum demands of third grade. Yes, for us, second grade is the place to be.

We teach in a suburban community whose families have the problems seen across our country in this decade. Our students come to us with a wide range of abilities and emotional demands. In the hectic rat race of the 1990s, children live with the tension between the very real needs of their parents and their own. Some come from intact homes where children are a family priority. Others carry the confusion and heartbreak of a severed family. Illness, death, and disability are not excluded from the lives of our students.

We have taught prekindergarten and first, second, third, and fourth grades. Together we share more than fifty years of experience as educators. Donna served as a reading specialist and Jane taught gifted and talented children. We have both been staff developers. We have taught through school closings, budget crunches, administrative restructuring, and local political battles.

During those years our belief that all children want to learn has remained unaltered. We have constantly revisited the question, How can we best help children acquire knowledge? And our theories have been continually updated based on our observations, reading, and discussions with our students, our colleagues, and each other. Our most vital source of information remains the classroom. If the wisdom shared by others in a workshop fails to spark the healthy, energized interest we thought would occur, we take our cue from our students and rethink the advice. We want our readers to do the same.

A critical component of our evolving classroom practices is our school. We are surrounded by colleagues who love what they do, enjoy spending their days with children, and are dedicated educators. We may not all share the same teaching styles, but we respect each other and our professional differences. We value collaboration and celebrate together with a hoot and a holler when a child makes a long-awaited stride. Our building administrator, Dan Sullivan, conveys to us a trust and admiration for the work we do. His support and faith grant us permission to teach as well as we might. Our language arts guide, math scope and sequence, and science guide are defined so that the execution and details are left to us. We can match the interests and needs of our present class with the system's guidelines. That framework contains the autonomy we need to be creative, thoughtful practitioners. We know we must think on the job and that our job is thinking.

Before we make it sound too simple, we must add that we have played a role in shaping and writing the system-wide curriculum guides. When we worked as staff development teachers, we also headed curriculum teams who studied, had long discussions, and finally drafted documents that allowed for teacher/student flexibility. Those years of leadership were both exciting and difficult. There will always be unresolved issues about the best ways to help emergent readers and writers.

Like other teachers, the way we work with our second graders has been influenced by the larger educational community. Three major ideas, especially, affect our philosophy and practice. We are convinced that the learning landscape in our rooms would be very different without these recent developments.

Teachers as Researchers

The idea that research could be carried out by a teacher during the course of the teaching day sounded far-fetched. Research was done at universities and involved control groups and statistics. Nancie Atwell, Lucy McCormick Calkins, and others demonstrated that powerful professional learning can take place when teachers conduct research within the context of their classrooms. Adopting the ethnographic research techniques of anthropology, teacher-researchers unleashed a force of learning and discovery.

Collaborating with fine teachers as we learned how to incorporate new learning into practice has deepened our understanding while generating new questions to be answered. New questions have pushed us toward a major influence on our lives as educators: becoming teacher-researchers.

Donna invited teachers in our school system to join a teacher-research group after she worked with Lucy McCormick Calkins for two years as the recipient of a Gould Foundation grant. Ten of us met every other Tuesday after school. We brought journals filled with observations, questions, and concerns and shared our thoughts, microwave popcorn, and support for each other as we learned more about reading and writing in our classrooms. We read books and articles written by other teacher-researchers. We invited Kathy Lauterbach, a teacher from Katonah-Lewisboro, New York, to talk with us about her research in the fifth grade. Her one year of research experience was enviable to neophytes.

As we searched and learned together after school, we began to believe in the potential for learning together in the classroom. We started to share research with our students, ask their opinions, and interview them individually. We included them in decisions that, we discovered, should have been theirs to make all along.

When we asked young writers what had helped them the most with their writing, they gave us lucid and thoughtful responses. We were astounded. We couldn't wait for our next meeting to share the insightful student comments. Why didn't we know students had such knowledge?

Becoming teacher-researchers changed our stance in the classroom. We had become inquirers who wanted the voices of students to inform our work. Thus, our journals are always somewhere in the room with a pen stuck through the spiral waiting to be called into service. Our students know that we, too, are learners who record what is happening in our lives and reflect on that information to keep each day productive and purposeful.

Language and Literature

In the past ten years, new information about written and oral language and the expanded role of literature has had a major influence on our teaching and learning. A classroom rich with books, magazines, and other forms of the printed word invites everyone into Frank Smith's "Literacy Club." With a wide range of reading materials in the classroom, students expect to be readers. Their attempts at early reading and writing are welcomed in school with the same enthusiasm as their first spoken words and sentences.

The whole language movement empowered teachers to open the world of literature to students long before they could decode. New beliefs and attitudes about how children acquire language have encouraged teachers to offer students what they love: the magic of story. Teachers of younger children have always read to their classes, but now students can find the magic for themselves through language activities that fling wide the windows and permit enchantment to enter.

The workshop concept has been extended to include reading. A visitor, unfamiliar with the present-day schoolroom, would have difficulty deciding whether reading or writing was in progress.

Choice is crucial to both reading and writing. Gone are the Bluebirds and Cardinals of the round table. Text sets, multiple copies of trade books, picture books, magazines, and poetry abound in the classroom. Response groups have replaced reading groups, and reference charts filled with student thinking decorate our walls. There is a dynamic energy evident in the classroom as children read, write, and discuss books and writing with each other and their teacher.

Learning Is Social

"Learning is a consequence of community," Dixie Goswami said during a writing conference at Fairfield University. That phrase resounded in our minds. We also heard David, Roger, and Edie Johnson describe cooperative learning. The more we listened, read, and reflected on our own collaborative learning, the stronger our pledge to let children work and learn together.

Short and Burke write in *Creating Curriculum* that "We need learning environments where we can see others actively learning and can engage in many collaborative dialogues about our ideas and experience" (1991, 15).

Of the four langauge modes, talk has often been the unwelcome stepchild in the classroom. We used to think of reading, writing, and listening as silent, and talk as noisy. Since we've begun to respect the role of talk in the classroom, we realize that reading and writing are not silent acts, either. Allowing for conversations in the classroom has transformed how children interact and learn and has changed the way we view ourselves and our role as educators. "We don't learn from higgledy-piggledy events as they strike our senses; we learn from events as we interpret them, and one of the main ways of interpreting them is by talking about them—by giving them shape in language" (Britton 1982, 98). Talk is the mortar that shapes and strengthens the classroom community.

Yes, there are times when silence is necessary and welcome, but it is not the main melody. Children, like adults, need to talk with each other to make meaning of their lives. They need to have their own voices heard and to hear the voices of their classmates. "Social interventions bring about the growth of learning," writes Frank Smith (1992, 435). We know this is true from our collaboration with colleagues. We also know it is true from observing and talking with young learners in the classroom.

Our work as teacher-researchers, the expanded role of literature and language in the classroom, and the acceptance of the social nature of learning pushed us to reconsider life in the second grade. We needed to rethink our purposes and practices and enlarge our view of the scholarly activity possible for seven-year-olds. What could and should be the scope of work for the young readers and writers? How could we best assist them to make meaning in their reading and writing lives?

When Jane retired to work as a consultant while Donna continued in her second-grade classroom, we decided it was time to write about our experiences and attempt to answer these and other questions. We have had sustained opportunity to collaborate and discuss our belief systems. We had already learned that our differences could be braided together to make a fuller whole. Although we have written as if the events occurred in a single classroom, we have had separate rooms and responsibilities. In our teaching, and in writing this book, we have always worked in close collaboration.

We hope our book provides some answers as it raises further questions. Our thoughts should not limit your thinking. They are not a set of prescriptions for how to teach reading and writing. On the contrary, we know teachers must resist prescriptive shortcuts. The appendix contains lists and charts that we have used for reading and writing classrooms. View them as a possible first draft for your own purposes. They may spark your thinking and aid in planning and organizing your reading and writing workshops.

We found that by taking charge of our professional lives, we were able to invite students to be active and inquiring learners along with us. The excitement and joy in our classrooms increased with the quantity and quality of the learning. The results have given us the conviction and courage to share our thinking and practices with you.

References

Britton, James. 1982. *Prospect and Retrospect: Selected Essays of James Britton*. Portsmouth, NH: Boynton/Cook.

Kline, Suzy. 1992. *Herbie Jones and the Dark Attic*. New York: G. P. Putnam's.

Short, Kathy G., and Carolyn Burke. 1991. *Creating Curriculum: Teachers and Students as a Community of Learners*. Portsmouth, NH: Heinemann.

Smith, Frank. 1992. "Learning to Read: The Never-Ending Debate." *Phi Delta Kappan* 73 (February): 432–41.

Second Grade: A New Look

ᏋᏮ On the first day of school Donna asked her second graders to write two reasons why children go to school. She thought if they generated a list it would reassure them that they had abandoned summer vacation for a worthy purpose. She was careful to explain that there were no right or wrong answers.

"Why don't you look in your book?" Richard asked from his seat nearby.

"Which book?" Donna asked. His sun-fresh seven-year-old face looked so serious.

"In first grade my teacher had a book with all the answers in it," Richard stated boldly.

Donna assured Richard that the class would think of good reasons and that they didn't need an answer book, but his words stuck in her mind: "My teacher had a book with all the answers in it."

Richard's view of school and learning characterizes a traditional view of school. The teacher has all the answers written down in a book. The job of the student is to learn what is in this book. For years classrooms encouraged children to see teaching and learning in that same dysfunctional dimension.

Traditional second-grade classrooms defined the learner in a restricted way. To succeed, the child had to listen, follow directions, and complete assignments. The script was in place. Much of it was written by publishers or curriculum committees. The teacher had questions to ask and curriculum to cover.

In September students would check how many pages were in the basal workbook. They could predict what was ahead. They also knew they were to complete the workbook pages independently and in silence. Right answers were the measure of success. The teacher was responsible for telling them if they did well or not.

Second grade was considered a year of transition and consolidation. Readers no longer needed to sound out words or subvocalize. They refined reading skills and moved into longer books with emphasis on comprehension and increased vocabulary. Printing diminished in size, the middle dotted line on the paper became superfluous, and writers gained fluency as they were able to focus on more than letter formation and spelling. By the end of second grade, students were to be ready for the academic demands of third grade, launching into the serious content of school. Learning to read and write was accomplished and the student was expected to use those abilities to learn all that the curriculum outlined.

In the mid 1980s as district reading and writing teachers in grades kindergarten through six, we inherited a writing program. We visited classes each week, read a story or poem, and gave students a writing prompt. After a few months of giving story starters to second graders and then racing around the room in response to waving hands to spell words and encourage reluctant writers, we had helped to create classrooms of dependent writers. Students waited to be given their topic, to brainstorm ideas, for directions to set up their paper, to have words spelled, and to be told if their story was long enough. The dependency of students was debilitating for both teachers and learners. We had helped to foster their dependency by implementing the mandated writing program. In retrospect, writing time was more a lesson in following directions than it was a lesson in writing. For us, writing instruction had become a lesson in frustration. The notion of writing workshop was just a whisper on the wind but we began to talk with teachers about articles we were reading that suggested students could select their own topics and work at their own pace. The concept of choice seemed developmentally appropriate and we were ready to try it.

Reading practices were a mirror image of our writing assignments. Teachers felt children were not ready to choose their own reading material and that reading needed to be taught in a specific sequence that was followed by all children. Individual needs were met by providing a faster or slower pace through the same materials. If the teacher used trade books for a reading group, the accompanying questions were a check to see if the child had read and understood the book, much like questions for basal readers.

A reading lesson ignored the experience of readers and their investment in the book. The words in the book had a clear message and the teacher knew what that message was. As Richard already knew, the student reader was to figure out the interpretation in the teacher's answer book. There *was* a right answer.

Life in a traditional second-grade classroom was predictable and stable. A well-organized and experienced teacher knew how to keep three reading groups smoothly progressing through their assigned texts. Classroom management was rooted in the required seatwork of workbooks or duplicated pages and board work. Reading and writing seemed the province of teachers and schools. Students saw little connection to their own lifelong literacy. And then something remarkable happened. . . .

Maybe it was that some teachers grew bored reading the same basal story year after year with reading group after reading group. Or maybe it was the research of Don Graves and Lucy McCormick Calkins in Atkinson, New Hampshire, which revealed that young children have stories to tell and can write them down. Or maybe it was the teachers who saw a connection between the way children learn to talk and the way they learn to read and write. Whatever the seeds of change, they began to blow across oceans and across our continent and some teachers began to recognize exciting possibilities for the teaching of reading and writing. With professional reading, classroom research, conferences, and staff development workshops, a new paradigm gradually emerged. Our assumptions about young learners began to shift and expand.

In the past, administrative decisions have mandated what transpires in the classroom so most changes in education have come from the top down. The transitions in second grade and in the classrooms of other grades were different. They came largely from teachers—educators who wanted to work with children as readers and writers in authentic, real-world ways.

As teachers, we came to understand that when we give young learners a narrow performance definition, we assume that they are what we see. Offered broader possibilities, children surprise us with hidden abilities and talents. Jane remembers Marisa who sat and avidly read *Mr. Popper's Penguins* (Atwater 1992). She was captivated by the story. She giggled and laughed aloud completely unaware that everyone in the class was watching her. She decided to do research on penguins. She invited Rebecca and Alexis to help her make a list of what they had learned about penguins from this novel. Then they read several nonfiction books before writing and illustrating their own book, which they called *The Learning Book about Penguins.* Marisa, Rebecca, and Alexis had the opportunity and the time to pursue their interest in penguins. They demonstrated abilities to gather, organize, and synthesize information far beyond what Jane would have expected or requested.

How have the exciting changes in teaching and learning in the elementary grades reshaped the second grade? We will discuss three concepts that have inspired our work.

Higher Expectations

There is one statement we have stopped making or even thinking: "You need to do this now so you will be ready for third grade." Consider it. Is it a legitimate goal to gear young learners for the third grade? What a low standard. Isn't it better to prepare them for a life of reading, writing, and learning?

For many years we set the bar low for seven-year-olds. They read prescribed stories but did not need to make independent decisions about books. Worksheets told students what was important to know from a story. Young readers did not have to think deeply about what was read, nor did they have to think about what to read next. The teacher of the basal provided the next assignment. Usually, it was the next story in the reader.

We expect our students to have the habits of readers who know how to choose the books they want to read. Our reading program is structured to familiarize students with a wide variety of authors and genres. By the end of second grade our students have strong reading preferences and enter the library with enthusiasm and confidence. Paul is turned on by James Howe, Brian prefers biographies. Ashley loves Patricia Reilly Giff.

Children who have preferences are much more likely to read on their own. They have already discovered what does and what does not give them pleasure. They know how to avoid the dead end of trying to struggle through a book that is unsatisfactory. There are too many wonderful books in the world to settle for something we can't abide, and during the long course of their schooling students will have many books chosen for them. It is imperative that they can select enjoyable books when they want to settle in with a good read.

Asking second graders to be knowledgeable about reading preferences requires more reflection and self-knowledge. They know which classmates make good recommendations, which section of the library houses their kind of books, and which adults are reliable resources for good suggestions. Habitual readers know how to ferret out that next exciting book.

We expect our students to understand and use many reading strategies. We discuss making predictions, noticing clues, reading chapter titles, and relating stories to their own lives. Children reread, summarize, and use context to better understand the text. Second graders learn to use these and other strategies, which can then become lifelong tools.

Another habit of ambitious readers is reading for a variety of purposes. We expect our students to use reading to answer their questions about the world. Reading is more than a period of time in the school day: it is a way to discover fascinating information, to be transported to another galaxy, or to spend time with a literary character who feels like a friend. We celebrate when Bridget initiates a project on dolphins and spends her weekend organizing and typing up what she has learned. We are joyful to hear Courtney and Hallie talking about Laura and why she wished her hair looked like her sister Mary's. (Wilder 1971). We smile at the serious discussion between Jacqueline and Katherine about learning to write cursive. They cannot understand Muggie Maggie's resistance (Cleary 1990). When reading moves from an assigned story to being the habit of a learner, we know we have not asked too much of our students. Rather, we have tapped into their human desire to understand and make sense of the world.

Our expectations are also higher in the way we ask young readers to respond to literature. Fill-in-the-blank worksheets and single-word answers solicit little information about the reader's thinking. Assignments that challenge students to express their thoughts on paper up the ante. Asking students to compose the questions for group discussions demands more of them as readers. Their involvement with the text deepens when we give them tasks that were formerly done by the teacher: asking the questions, highlighting passages with special language, or selecting difficult vocabulary words that need discussion. With our continual modeling and guidance, second-grade readers accept the challenge and surprise themselves with their ability to think in sustained ways about a book.

Another significant change that reflects our higher expectations is that we assume everyone will belong to the literacy club. The bell curve has become irrelevant. We see everyone discussing books together, sharing ideas, and becoming excited about reading and writing.

The hierarchy of former classrooms where a few talented first-draft writers gloried in the spotlight has been transformed into an environment where writers support and encourage each other. Group shares celebrate the efforts of writers at all levels. Children appreciate the work of the writer and applaud the accomplishments of others.

Our expectations are based on what it is we want these children to be doing as joyfully literate adults. What knowledge, skills, strategies, attitudes, abilities, and habits of the mind will they need? We imagine our students as we would have them become and try to keep that end clearly in our thoughts. We try to focus on the big picture: Where will they be in twenty years? in thirty years? What will they need to be successful, responsible, and thoughtful citizens?

Expanded Opportunities

We expect students to assume more responsibility for their own learning and, for our part, we try to provide more opportunities for them to show us their wide range of abilities and interests. We structure our reading and writing program so there is a broader definition of success.

During one writing workshop, Ashley and Sophie team up to write about a valentine party. Brent and Bryan write an action-packed story of six boys who are ninjas. Sarah writes her autobiography beginning at the time she leaves Korea to be adopted in the United States. These authors choose a topic that they care about, topics that they know well enough to write with authority and confidence.

Students now have the opportunity to decide on their topic, to determine if their work needs revision, to define the audience, and to decide if their final product should be published. The nature of writing workshop allows them to work on a piece much longer than they did in traditional second-grade classrooms. With our former story starter program, children wrote their story in one period and recopied it the next. Decisions about topic, revision, editing, and publishing belonged to the teacher. Students could remain passive and still complete the assignment.

The length of time a piece is in progress varies tremendously. Some students, especially in the beginning of the year, like to knock off a simple story each writing time. Philip had a folder full of stories about skateboarding, scuba diving, soccer, and tennis. Each short book followed the same format, allowing him to solidify his skills and feel successful. Bridget and Kristin worked feverishly on "The Best Hallow-een Ever" for at least eight weeks. Their use of dialogue, description, and action impressed all of us during group share. Sean wrote "The Great American Army" over a period of three months. His voluminous text was filled with a myriad of details and facts about the army that none of us knew. We sat awed during successive shares as he proudly read the next installment.

Seven- and eight-year-olds have a variety of likes and dislikes. Both reading and writing workshop provide the opportunity for students to tap into their personal interests as they read and write about topics that intrigue them. Because most children enjoy new challenges, we may suddenly witness an exciting departure from the old mold in which a student has been functioning.

Jane began to write a reflective journal when she was working on staff development. In an entry after returning to the classroom she notes:

> It is so good to have my own classroom again. If I were still working with students in the classrooms of other teachers, I might not have noticed Kelly. She is a different person during reading and writing workshops. She is so in charge, so confident. She makes decisions and carries them out. She smiles a lot. She talks with authority with her classmates. Away from reading and writing workshop she is passive and doesn't seem motivated. She waits for others to take the lead. She comes to life only when the learning is structured as process and choices are available with appropriate activities for a child her age.

In February Jane read *Hot Fudge* (Howe 1990) and the class made fudge to celebrate her birthday. Joe, a special-needs student, was so enchanted by the story and—perhaps—by the fudge, that he talked his mother into taking him to the local bookstore to purchase *Bunnicula* (Howe 1980). His interest was further increased by this second book, and he became the proud owner of *Howliday Inn* (Howe 1983). Joe talked to the group about James Howe, sometimes laughing as he read from the book. He expressed the hope that he would be able to write in such a funny manner. No one else in the class was reading this author, but Joe was happily pursuing his own interests.

In *Experiment with Fiction* (1989), Don Graves writes about Joe's kind of reading.

> When children read an author as a writer, they more naturally integrate an overall sense of balance, language selection, and the relationship of part to whole needed to keep a piece moving into their own composing frame. Some children learn best by concentrating on reading one author and composing one story over a long period of time. Such reading can't be forced; yet when a child pursues that one author to learn the author's composing secrets, a new kind of learning takes place that is seldom seen in school curricula. (pp. 59–60)

Second-grade writers find their own pace and rhythm. The opportunity is there to read or write a short wordless book or the great American novel. We urge young readers and authors to do their very best. The broad continuum of very best continues to intrigue us.

The intense peer life of seven and eight year olds is served by the expanded opportunities of both reading and writing workshop. We structure blocks of time when students can work together. This enhances their learning through social interactions. Second graders are capable of staying on task when they work with a partner or in a small group. In his group, Jamie played the role of policeman as he kept everyone on task. It felt better to him when the group was doing what he thought was expected of it. He often reminded others, as they got off the subject, what they were supposed to be doing and because he did it in such a nice way, his classmates took his reminders seriously.

Students have opportunities to share their work within our class and with wider audiences. Jane's class worked with Hilda Rhodes's kindergarten class for several years. Second graders became the mentors and tutors for the emerging writers in kindergarten. When Hilda's former students began second grade in Jane's class, they had an already firm and expanded view of themselves as writers and mentors. They were eager to revisit the scene of their own kindergarten days.

Expanded student opportunities mean that students may choose to publish a piece or to save it in their writing folder. They may decide if their story would work better as a play and change the story into a script. The possibilities are limited only by their imagination and creativity. The flow of ideas stays abundant and fresh when students share what they are working on and what adult authors have written.

There are many more opportunities to talk with classmates than there used to be. We understand and foster the need to think out loud so that thinking can be confirmed or clarified by peers. Talking about writing also makes explicit many aspects that previously went unnoticed. As Arielle and Kat talk together about their rabbit book, they realize their main character lacks a problem to solve. As they work, heads bent over their writing, they remind each other of the important elements of a good story. The opportunity for conversations, whether about writing or about life, allows young writers to feel they are members of the classroom literacy club.

Readers in our rooms choose their books from our classroom collections, from the school library, from home, or from the many books we bring regularly from the public library. They are not locked into a track that predetermines what they read and with whom. Their choice of books often decides their reading partner or group. They surprise us with the unexpected groups that decide to work together and do so successfully.

Providing increased opportunities for them to take charge of their reading and writing gives them a sense of their own potential. They accept the additional work it involves and can become indignant at the thought that they are not capable of making important reading and writing decisions.

A Dynamic Curriculum

We are able to offer expanded opportunities to young readers and writers because we are not limited by a tightly scripted curriculum. The goals of our townwide scope and sequence are broadly defined to encourage children to become lifelong readers and writers. We have the authority to let our curriculum be responsive to the felt need of the class. We do not have to complete a prescribed basal program where the educational decisions were made by a distant publisher who has never met the unique individuals in our classrooms. We are free to pursue the scholarly activities that we judge our students need or find engaging.

In February the children learned Lilian Moore's poem "Ground Hog Day." After several repetitions, Nathan conceived the idea of turning it into a play, which took on a life of its own. As narrator, he became very dramatic, holding a microphone in his hand and introducing the idea of Groundhog Day with Puxatawny Phil, the "renowned" Pennsylvania groundhog. Props were added, including an imaginary video camera recording Phil's activities.

Another example of the dynamic curriculum occurred when Jane used a short nonfiction article on owls for a reading lesson. Michael brought his "Owls" *Zoo Book* (Biel 1990) for class inspection. Jane found an article on the resurgence of owls in New Jersey. She read *Owl Moon* aloud (Yolen 1987), and the group discussed where the author got her writing ideas and what additional information about owls they had learned. The same book provoked discussion about the illustrations by John Schonherr and the class related them to the illustrations of a talented class member. Some children began trying their hands at owl illustrations. *The Man Who Could Call Down Owls* (Bunting 1984) provoked thoughts about human relations with animals and whether the story could possibly be true. Using the *Zoo Book* as a source, students measured the size of different owls, putting tape and labels on the carpet to make the measurements more concrete. Our colleague Pat Beasley, who was working on staff development in science, suggested lessons about form and function. Children examined why the eyes of owls are fixed in their sockets and cannot move. They noted that owls can rotate their heads up to 270 degrees. They looked at the shape of owl beaks and discussed their usefulness in catching prey.

Repeated examination of the changes in the red maple tree outside Jane's classroom led to many integrated activities. Some ideas came from us and some were initiated by students. We read and discussed *A Tree Is Nice* (Udry 1956), *Once There Was a Tree* (Romanova 1985), and *The Giving Tree* (Silverstein 1964). Susanna attempted her own story about a tree, inspired by the authors of the books we read. Her tree lived forever, which befitted seven-year-old thought. We estimated the circumference of our red maple after practicing with round objects in the room and went outside to measure it. We turned *Ghost Eye Tree* (Martin and Archambault 1985) into a much-cherished and oft-repeated readers' theater piece (see the section on readers' theater in chapter 8). Students searched for poems about trees in Jane's poetry collection, finding "Trees" (Behn 1968), "Tree House" (Silverstein 1988) and "Counting-Out Rhyme" (Millay 1967). Some were inspired to try writing poems of their own.

Last September Donna stopped by the local library the weekend before school started. Her room was ready for the enthusiastic invasion the following week and she wanted to choose books for the first author study. While considering different possibilities, she stopped. It was as if she were trying to buy back-to-school clothes for young strangers. She had no idea what would pique their interest, what authors they had studied already, and what topics interested them. She could end up with an ill-fitting collection of books. A welcoming postcard had asked them to bring a favorite book to class the first day. Her classroom already had over five hundred books her own children had outgrown, friends had donated, or she had received with bonus points through book clubs. Donna decided that waiting to choose the books would honor the children more. They could tell her what books to get. The books would feel more like carefully chosen presents rather than impersonal grab-bag gifts.

Favorite books brought to school on the first day have helped us choose books for an author study. Jamie brought *The Relatives Came* (Rylant 1985). A stir was created in the classroom with memories of visits to and from relatives that was the perfect prompt for an author study. Jane had written to Ms. Rylant and had letters to share with her students. The *Henry and Mudge* series (Rylant 1987–93) became classroom favorites and everyone waited breathlessly for the possibility of a new book. Students compared and contrasted her works as they discussed her versatility, prolific creativity, and use of special language.

Higher expectations, expanded opportunities, and the dynamic curriculum have combined to change the way we think about our classrooms and our students. We do not mourn the days of story starters and basal readers. We find tremendous excitement and satisfaction in the new second grade. Our students feel more confident and empowered. They like taking responsibility for their learning. Excited about new ideas and new skills, we witness their increasing attention to detail in the service of large concepts and their lengthening attention span as the year progresses.

We now turn to look at the developmental hallmarks that characterize these seven- and eight-year-olds. There is a significant fit between higher expectations, expanded opportunities, a dynamic curriculum, and these developmental markers. This match between new practices and the nature of the seven-year-old creates an energized pulse in the new second grade.

References

Atwater, Richard. 1992. *Mr. Popper's Penguins*. New York: Dell.

Behn, Harry. 1968. "Trees." In *Time for Poetry*, edited by May Hill Arbuthnot and Shelton L. Root, Jr. Glenview, IL: Scott, Foresman.

Biel, Timothy L. 1990. "Owls," *Zoo Books* (Mankato, MN: Creative Education), entire volume.

Bunting, Eve. 1984. *The Man Who Could Call Down Owls*. New York: Macmillan.

Cleary, Beverly. 1990. *Muggie Maggie*. New York: Morrow Junior Books.

Graves, Donald H. 1989. *Experiment with Fiction*. Portsmouth, NH: Heinemann.

Howe, Deborah, and James Howe. 1980. *Bunnicula: A Rabbit-Tale of Mystery*. New York: Avon.

Howe, James. 1983. *Howliday Inn*. New York: Avon.

———. 1990. *Hot Fudge*. New York: Morrow Junior Books.

Martin, Bill, Jr., and John Archambault. 1985. *The Ghost Eye Tree*. New York: Holt, Rinehart and Winston.

Millay, Edna St. Vincent. 1967. "Counting Out Rhyme." In *Reflections on a Gift of Watermelon Pickle . . . and Other Modern Verse*, edited by Stephen Dunning, Edward Lueders, and Hugh Smith. New York: Lothrop, Lee & Shephard.

Moore, Lilian. 1983. "Ground Hog Day." In *The Random House Book of Poetry for Children*, edited by Jack Prelutsky. New York: Random House.

Romanova, Natalia. 1985. *Once There Was a Tree*. New York: Dial Books for Young Readers.

Rylant, Cynthia. 1985. *The Relatives Came*. New York: Bradbury Press.

———. 1987–93. *Henry and Mudge* series. New York: Bradbury Press.

Silverstein, Shel. 1964. *The Giving Tree*. New York: Harper & Row.

———. 1988. "Tree House." In *Sing a Song of Popcorn*, edited by Beatrice Schenk de Regniers. New York: Scholastic.

Udry, Janice. 1956. *A Tree Is Nice*. New York: Harper & Row.

Wilder, Laura Ingalls. 1971. *Little House in the Big Woods*. New York: HarperCollins.

Yolen, Jane. 1987. *Owl Moon*. New York: Philomel Books.

Smiles with Spaces: Developmental Considerations 2

❧ Jesse had been working hard to loosen his upper right incisor. As he approached his eighth birthday it was almost a matter of honor to be without that front tooth. But the tooth refused to budge and there was a slow shift in Jesse's thinking. Now it became important to have the tooth there.

When he arrived at school on his birthday morning, Jane inquired about the tooth. He replied, "I'm going to hang onto this tooth until I am as old as Grandma Alice. She's eighty-eight. Then I will say in a shaky, old man's voice, 'Look at my tooth!' "

You can often spot second graders by their smiles. A gap in the front signals a typical seven-year-old. And yet, all second graders are as individual as the course of their dental development. A personal rate of development, idiosyncracies, experiences to date, and family constellation all swirl together to create a delightful group of individuals with personal needs, desires, and preferences: "Every age, like every person, has it own unique individuality" (Ames and Haber 1985).

Each fall we reread *Your Seven Year Old* by Ames and Haber (1985). We remind ourselves of the salient points so that our transition back into the classroom can feel less rugged. During the summer our former second graders move on to the new world of third grade. At the same time, we must retrace our steps and be ready for the new crop of first-grade graduates. Each batch of fresh faces presents its own pleasures and peculiarities, but there are certain characteristics that we have come to expect. Understanding the complex nature of the second grader provides us with the patience and fortitude to love what we do and want to do it again.

September is a demanding month at school. Until the children establish relationships with us and with each other, life in that small space can be uneven at best. Each fall when we ask parents to write to us about their children, a key word used by many of them to describe their child is "sensitive." Yes, second graders are sensitive. Yet many have not yet developed a sensitivity to others. Their antennae are out as receptors, but they may only be tuned to their own channel. They are still learning how to forge friendships. We try to be aware of their emotional needs as they reach for friends and a strong relationship with their teacher in the intense social situation of a classroom.

Most second graders have moved to the stage of development where they can accept their role as a group member. There are often a few less-mature children who have difficulty sublimating their own needs for the good of the group. Beth had difficulty understanding the needs of others in the class. With her actions, she often divided the girls into groups, producing a we/they situation. Jane remembers the day when the girls returned from lunch recess all steamed up. Beth had planned a "production" of *The Wonderful Wizard of Oz*, had assigned parts to those who were to be included, and had told others they could not participate. The whole grandiose project was abandoned by Beth within the day, but the hurt feelings lingered.

Seven-year-olds may fall off their chairs and have trouble sitting still during group stories and discussions. Many seven-year-olds find it more demanding to sit quietly than they do to run and jump. More mature children of this age can sustain sitting and listening for long periods, but it is not their natural tendency and can leave them fatigued. Our classes sit spellbound listening to a story or a book. As the last page is turned, small body movements begin as students shift gears for the book discussion. They've reached their limit of immobility and silence.

Sitting still is not a high priority for us because we know that developmentally it is not an easy assignment for many beginning second graders. During reading and writing workshop we allow for movement, for walking around the room, for conversation, and for a quick change of activities because changes of pace and focus may lead to chunks of time when the quiet pursuit of personal work will be possible. Leah and Amy move to the corner to curl up and write together. Walt and Derek lean against the closet—legs stretched out.

Second graders have an energy that is marvelous to witness but they are poor judges of their own limits. They use their energy without sparing themselves until they are so drained they are ready to collapse.

Part of our job is to help students pace themselves and to even call a halt to activities when some feel they want to continue.

If left to their own inclinations, some would push on with a project past the point where they are satisfied with it. Then the tears may begin. We've learned to insist on putting work aside after a certain length of time as seven-year-olds cannot gauge their own fatigue. Ames and Haber remind us that their eyes tire easily and that they need to avoid staying too long with one task.

Arielle and Alex agreed to sort the books in the book corner. They began with gusto, removing all the bins and stacking the books in piles. It didn't seem necessary to completely clear the shelves, but the two eager beavers insisted they had a plan. When it was time to go to lunch, the books were still stacked on the floor. After recess, the two labored on during read-aloud time. About 1:30 Arielle came quietly over to Donna to whisper that she had a headache. Could someone else help in the book corner now?

This initial zest is a trademark of the second grader. They tackle a job, especially one they perceive to be unusual or prestigious (washing the dishes after a cooking project, scrubbing the tables and desktops), with unbounded energy. But their energy flags before the job, made elaborate by their imaginations, is completed. Seven-year-olds benefit from measured advice from the teacher to see tasks through. They sometimes exhaust themselves with complicated plans that have little chance of succeeding. We know these errors in judgment are harmless and provide experiences that are necessary for children to learn and grow.

Second graders are also worriers. Our students worry no one will like them, that they will be made fun of, that their parents like a sibling better. They may think others are mean to them or that the teacher picks on them. These dark thoughts, however, are mitigated by their budding ability to talk things over. They are developing an increasing reasonableness that allows them to listen to someone else's side of the story.

Rachel worried because she said she didn't have a best friend. As an only child, her parents had a heavy investment in her success and happiness. Her mom confided this worry to Jane, who had not yet detected this problem. Rachel was a bubbly, enthusiastic child who contributed a great deal to the class and seemed to be liked by everyone. As this worry persisted, her mom rightly felt it was an important part of Rachel's seven-year-old life. Rachel's need for a best friend created problems for Rachel herself, though not for others in the class.

The need for a small club of friendship can fester and may require delicate handling. Maggie wrote this letter in her journal to Donna in January:

> Dear Mrs. S.
>
> Some of the people in our class make me really mad when they talk about me. Whenever people talk about me I turn pale because I feel so bad. Please help me.

In March, Maggie wrote another letter:

> Dear Mrs. S.
>
> Kids are being really nice to me now and I feel a lot better because of a lot of things. My birthday is coming up and I'm getting a rabbit for my birthday. Next Wednesday I'm getting my rabbit, even though my birthday's March 25 but my mom said I could get it then and I'm so excited. I can't wait.

Children may perceive how others feel about them based on their current emotions. When these children are under the weather or vulnerable because of something that happened, it will take a while before they are able to put their anxiety aside and focus on class activities. Every class has its worry champions, those children who take everything to heart. These supersensitive children are especially tuned in to what they perceive as slights by others.

Lydia's functioning depends on how others treat her. She felt left out when she did not have her sticker book in school and a group of children were trading stickers during snack break. Lydia reported, "I hate when kids trade stickers. They yell, they shout, and they forget their friends." Lydia didn't like being ignored as sticker frenzy swept the room that day.

At some point during the year, sticker manufacturers capture our second graders. This year it was in March. Stickers are sorted by texture, size, or subject in their sticker books. Elaborate bargaining precedes trading. Girls are usually more attracted to stickers than boys, who are often more enticed by sports cards. But second graders love to be collectors. It could be erasers, trolls, coins, or markers. Their collections are squirreled away in a special place considered to be theirs alone. These collections seem to reflect a desire to be more distinct or individual, whether in school or at home.

When Sally and Amy were trading stickers, Sally thought that she could reverse the trade if she changed her mind. Amy thought the deal was done. She wanted to keep Sally's sunglasses sticker, which changed color at the touch. We needed a class meeting and a vote to decide if sticker trades were done deals or if you were allowed to change your mind. Once the rule was clear (they voted to allow a second chance to change their minds), the children were able to trade stickers and abide by the rule they had agreed upon.

In general, seven-year-olds have high standards and are serious about responsibilities. They want to do things right and they expect their classmates to do the same. One or two moral judges usually reside in each class who appoint themselves guardians of the rules. They are quick to point out when someone fails to follow an important class precept. Luke's role as guardian was also tied to a desire for perfection.

Second-grade students traditionally rub eraser holes in their papers in their search for perfection. As children begin projects, especially art projects that support reading and writing, a handful will need to start over more than once. Carol is never satisfied with her first effort. Arielle takes her artwork so seriously that if she is not pleased nothing anyone says can convince her that she should continue. We allow for their need to begin again and our guidance is directed toward learning to finish projects. They do become better about completing tasks as the year progresses.

John felt so inadequate about his art work that he would cover up his attempts so classmates could not see them, calling attention to himself in a very obvious way. Jane learned to ignore his behavior rather than try to cajole him to do illustration or to give him praise for his efforts. This strategy paid off as the children followed her lead. Later in the year John became more comfortable with himself about drawing and quietly began to try it again.

Seven-year-olds can be too optimistic about their own abilities. If we were to ask, "Who wants to climb that tree and touch the top branch?" most hands would go up before they stopped to think about the realities. If we ask who would like to take a note to Mrs. Rhodes, students who have no idea who Mrs. Rhodes is or where her room is located will eagerly volunteer. Second graders are willing to try almost anything that has not failed utterly for them in the past. David thought he could easily scoot to the top of an old maple tree to retrieve his kite. It took all our persuasive powers to convince him he was *not* climbing the tree. We were relieved to have a strong wind solve the problem later in the day.

Horizons are expanding for our students as they move from

concrete toward abstract thinking. The concrete child is very literal. When Donna began teaching second grade she soon realized her metaphorical thinking would not be appreciated. She talked about the exciting learning journey the class would take in second grade. Jarrett wanted to know if he could be the leader. Katie wanted to know if they should get in line. On the other hand, Jane found that some children were ready to learn about metaphors. When the piece was explained, Jacqueline latched onto the metaphorical language in "How to Eat a Poem" by Eve Merriam (1967) and studiously tried to think of metaphors for her own writing.

Still, some students are able to take only the concrete details from books. Early in September Jane read her class *Joe on Sunday* (Blundell 1987). In this picture book, Joe becomes a different animal each day, depending upon his behavior. For many children, however, the story made sense only on a literal level. Amy suggested that Joe wore different costumes each day. Paul thought that Joe only dreamed he could change every day. As children offered their ideas, Jane realized the limits to their explanations were age appropriate, but it was hard not to tell them her interpretation. When she tried the book again later in the year, she found that they saw it differently. This book gave her a glimpse of their concrete thinking that she needed to know. Book discussions can be like Rorschach tests, allowing teachers to see into the minds of children. The challenge is to accept that we cannot change thinking that is bound by development or experience; moving from the concrete to the abstract occurs at a strictly individual pace.

Several children in Jane's class read *The Shoeshine Girl* by Clyde Bulla (1988). In a reading response group the question was asked why Sarah Ida wanted to work with Al, the shoeshine man.

ASHLEY: Sarah Ida wanted to help because it made her feel better about herself. It made her feel she was a good person.
ANDREW: No, she did it to make her aunt mad so she would be sent home.
BRIAN: She did it because she wanted to.
RACHEL: I don't understand why she didn't just go home. That's what she wanted to do. She should argue with her aunt until she got the money for the train trip home.

The young readers viewed this story from points of view that ranged from concrete to inferential and self-centered to the meaning of the psychological and developmental issues. Our job is to model ways to think about stories, to nudge the thinking of the child who is moving toward the abstract, and to accept interpretations from those who have not yet made the transition.

This is a sober, thoughtful age. Sulking and worry are normal expressions of seven-year-old life. Their thought processes are more intense than they may appear on the surface. When asked in January what they wanted to learn in the new year, their written responses indicated an awareness and concern that wasn't immediately apparent.

SARAH: I would like to learn more about Art, what's going on in the world. Sometimes I wonder what's happening to the people in Somalia. I want to learn about other people.

ALEX: I want to learn more about animals and get better at math. I wonder how it feels to be a cat.

ROB: I want to learn about snakes, turtles, space, invisible things, how the world came.

ASHLEY: I would like to learn more about horses, whales, sharks, stars, our planet, pets, Antarctica, volcanoes, the sun, space, the forest, deer, bunnies, what's happening to our planet.

Second graders have a lot on their minds that cannot easily be detected during an active, fragmented class day. Life at home may be just as hectic as it is at school. These children, who often only have small snatches of adult attention at home because their parents are so busy, have a great need to use their energy in school in a more sustained way. They are accustomed to the sound bite but capable of much more. Channeling their interests in sports or animals toward reading and writing is successful when combined with a dependable routine and structure. If encouraged to expand, to do more, to be more thoughtful, they respond with characteristic bravado and surprise themselves with the success of their efforts.

In *Your Seven Year Old,* Ames and Haber note that the seven-year-old has "high days and forgetting-everything days. An aware teacher will shift her intellectual fare on these different days" (1985, 88). Recognizing these swings in our classrooms, our expectation is not a smooth stair-step progression to maturity.

Tears serve as a barometer of the stress level. "Seven year olds normally do cry at every, or even no provocation. The typical seven revels in his gloom," write Ames and Haber (120). Some children are more susceptible to tears than others. Crying does increase prior to holidays and vacations. When children are tired or emotions are heightened, we see more quivering lips and know it is time for the patience and understanding these fragile souls require. Seven-year-olds can lose their composure over items of questionable value to adults, such as damage to a treasured and chewed eraser or a pencil stub, and we need to provide them with the emotional support they deserve.

As seven-year-olds move toward independence, adults are still sought at times of anxiety. Although listening and placating may not always come at convenient moments, these acts are an important part of working with students this age. These children depend on adults for assistance when they need it. Some of them have not yet learned to solve social problems by themselves and need to be taught the skills for doing so. We suggest, we model, and we send them back for another round of conciliation and mediation.

Conflict resolution can take a big chunk out of the days when emotions are running high. But most children are able to wait their turn to explain their side of an argument. Our second graders are dependable and aware of fairness issues. They can be trusted to remember and report when they have had a turn at the computer or with the class ball. They need the classroom to be a fair and consistent place. We use class lists a great deal to ensure that everyone has a chance to take the ball outside at recess, that jobs are rotated, that privileges such as being the line leader are evenly distributed. Seven-year-olds like to take responsibility and hope for respect from their peers and from adults.

Second graders pride themselves on having passed through kindergarten and first grade. In their third year at school, they want more independence and stature. Katharine announced to her mother in October, "You can't tell me what to do. I'm in second grade now." This attitude is also evident when Amanda decides she is now Mandy and Jonathan becomes Jon. We've learned to check with parents before bestowing nicknames. Some parents have strong preferences and request that Matthew not become Matt.

Students of this age have difficulty grasping the steps of a process that leads to a finished product. Donna began "learning adventures"—research projects—with her class. Shortly after she explained the procedure to the group and as the children were gathering materials to begin, Emily stated, "I'm finished." This was a surprise to everyone, especially Donna. She realized Emily was unable to visualize the process or what work it entailed. But, once Donna had again explained the process, Emily worked happily and hard over the next few weeks to complete her project.

When Heidi Hayes Jacobs spoke to our district staff, she commented that at the primary level there can be an emotional age range from two to twenty. We could immediately think of the child in our class who sometimes acted like a tired two-year-old and the child who was almost mature enough to have her own apartment. This vast range is one of the challenges of teaching second grade.

Gender differences are noticeable at this age. During writing workshop girls may write stories about adventures and perhaps even romance. Using animals as characters is another female characteristic. Boys love to draw mazes and weapons and to tell stories about ships, castles, or bad guys.

The girls seem more mature than the boys in their responses to assignments. They are often able to sit longer and focus better. They love the fine motor tasks involved in writing and illustrating. This may also be true for boys, though often their fine motor development is slower and they may need part of the year to grow into the enjoyment of these tasks.

About spring of the year boys and girls seem to discover each other in a new way. It is a healthy interest that can turn silly. Sometimes, however, it is more than they can handle, especially if complicated by influences of older children. At the end of February Donna found these notes on the floor of the classroom: "Mark has a krush on Sue," and "You are being mean. You no I olwes for give you. Why don't you no how I feel." These notes capture the essence of two major social concerns of the second grader at this time of year. Knowing these concerns, we plan for flexible social groups in our reading and writing programs to facilitate the development of relationships. Opportunities to work together and gain respect help seven- and eight-year-olds come to terms with their natural feelings of slight discomfort about the opposite sex: "Learning is social rather than solitary" (Smith 1992, 432). We try to structure our classrooms so that we can enhance the natural sociability of our students.

For a seven- or eight-year-old the adult in the classroom is someone to be admired and followed with devotion but not blindly. They will try hard to fulfill the teacher's expectations and do what is asked. This is a strength for both students and teachers in trying to teach and learn concepts, to achieve a classroom community, and to work toward guidelines and structures for behavior.

At the same time, second graders like to have their secrets about both their peer life and their feelings, which they keep separate from their relationships with us. Ashley and Vanessa came in from the playground whispering to each other, obviously upset about something. Jane offered help. They looked at each other with dismayed expressions. "Never mind," said Vanessa emphatically. Jane's translation of this statement was, "We'll solve this problem ourselves."

Seven-year-olds find it very exciting to meet adults they know. Our students are thrilled to see us out of the school context. At the grocery store or the mall we take on star qualities as they rush over to greet us. We find it endearing the way they wave excitedly to their parents as they enter the gym for the holiday performance. It has been less than an hour since they said good-bye at the bus stop—but they react as if they've just been reunited with a member of their family after a wagon trip along the Oregon Trail.

We began this chapter with a story about teeth. The loss of teeth somehow signals the time when children begin to focus on their own individuality. We often see flashes of real originality, followed by conformity that can be surprising. The lid is on, the lid is off. The mercury rises and falls. But as the permanent teeth appear, our students are growing into their more mature selves. We get glimpses of what we can expect to see when they are adults. Our job is to tap into these more-adult flashes. As they evolve, we hope they will become reflective adults capable of contributions to their ever-enlarging world.

References

Ames, Louise Bates, and Carol Chase Haber, 1985. *Your Seven Year Old*. New York: Delacorte Press.

Baum, Frank L. 1987. *The Wonderful Wizard of Oz*. New York: William Morrow.

Blundell, Tony. 1987. *Joe on Sunday*. New York: Dial Books for Young Readers.

Bulla, Clyde. 1988. *Shoeshine Girl*. New York: The Trumpet Club.

Merriam, Eve. 1967. "How to Eat a Poem." In *Reflections on a Gift of Watermelon Pickle . . . and Other Modern Verse*, edited by Stephen

Dunning, Edward Lueders, and Hugh Smith. New York: Lothrop, Lee & Shepard.

Smith, Frank. 1992. "Learning to Read: The Never-Ending Debate." *Phi Delta Kappan* 73 (February): 432–41.

Beginning with Grit and Grace

3

🐚 We sat on the beach anticipating the start of another school year. An excited young voice announced, "That's Mrs. Fraser." Marisa, in her damp bathing suit, held Stephanie's hand as she introduced us. Marisa was an about-to-be third grader, a graduate. Stephanie was entering Jane's class in a few weeks. "I can't wait for school to start," said Stephanie, reflecting the view of many seven-year-olds. For them, it was time.

We, too, feel a restlessness at the end of summer. Our internal clocks tell us the time is approaching and we know that so much has to be done that those last days of summer will fly by. We are getting ready for new challenges, for the intellectual stimulation of our professional lives. School begins for us long before the Tuesday after Labor Day, our traditional starting date for teachers. Thoughts of new students drift in and out on a summer day like the gentle waves.

An anxiety dream also announces that a new school year is near. When Donna returned to the classroom after over a decade in other educational roles, her anxiety dreams offered humorous scenarios of what can go wrong. In one dream, she was late to school. As she rushed into a classroom stacked high with large cardboard cartons, the custodian stood at the chalkboard calmly teaching about fractions. In another dream she was a student teacher with a different class assigned to each corner of the room. Whether we are veterans or new to teaching, we swap our dreams and laugh together. They are a normal part of anticipating the big day—the first of the school year.

August signals a time for reflection. We reread the journals from previous years searching for new clues and old thoughts about how to organize and structure life in the classroom. We make resolutions to ourselves and to the unknown bright-eyed faces that will soon cross the thresholds of our classrooms. Renewed after the summer break, we rededicate ourselves to being the best we can be.

Our aspirations are high and our list of goals is long. Among them we plan to

- create an environment that is supportive, trusting, and respectful;
- keep in mind what students value as we listen to and learn from them;
- accept students on their own terms;
- communicate an excitement for learning;
- build on strengths;
- use a sense of humor;
- be positive and savor success;
- be explicit and consistent;
- deal with each situation in the way it deserves; and
- see the big picture while focusing on necessary details.

We bring these goals into sharper focus as we start down a familiar trail with new traveling companions. It is important to stop and think about what makes a difference in our daily teaching lives even if some pledges seem second nature after many years in the classroom. We again ask ourselves, What conditions do second graders need to grow and thrive?

During the summer we begin to cover bulletin boards, write poems on large chart paper, and do the myriad of tasks that ensure smooth sailing on the first few critical days. This chapter looks at what we prepare before school begins and what we do in the classroom with our second graders to get the year off to a winning start. Woven through both sections are decisions that will influence the rest of the school year.

We estimate it takes a week to get ourselves ready for the fall invasion. The school secretary holds the key to many important details. She organizes the school handbook that contains our schedules, class lists, and other pertinent information. A few years ago the handbook was not available until the faculty meeting the morning before school started. Since many of us have changed our teaching styles over the past decade, our principal, Dan Sullivan, understands that we need the information earlier. He appreciates that our attention to detail facilitates a smooth beginning.

This chapter spells out the things we do to ensure a well-paced start. It also includes some of the journal entries Donna wrote as she made the transition back into the classroom after being a staff development teacher and having a sabbatical year.

Before School Begins
Some jobs can be easily accomplished in the quiet of August. Having these things under our belts helps us feel prepared to give our full attention to our new students. Our preparations are not complete until we have done certain tasks.

Becoming Familiar with a New Class
Learning the names of our new students even before we meet them is important to us. Several jobs we do before school starts help us familiarize ourselves with the twenty to twenty-five new names. Later we will put faces and detailed knowledge with those names as we get to know our new fellow learners.

Postcards to Students . . . . We send a note to children welcoming them to second grade. We mail the notes about a week before school begins. This year's postcard read:

> August 25
>
> Dear Josh,
>   Welcome to second grade. We will have a lot of fun as we learn together this year.
>   The first day of school please bring a healthy snack and a favorite book.
>   Enjoy the last week of summer.
>
> *Mrs. Fraser*

The request to bring a book sends a message about the role of literature in our classroom lives. The postcard bridges the end of summer and the approaching school year, inviting each student to bring a piece of home to school.

We phrase the short hand-printed card so that most students can read it. When Jordy was in fourth grade, he told Jane that he still had his postcard in a drawer where he kept his special things. During a book discussion in December, Paul related the book to the one he had brought the first day. He added that he liked to reread his postcard.

Class List Sign . . . . Once we have written the new names on postcards and stamped and mailed the cards, we write these names again on large chart paper to display outside the classroom door. The sign announces that the room belongs to all its members. It has been our experience that at least one child wants to be called DeeJay, not David, or Tommy and not Thomas. We check with office records or former teachers, trying to make the list as accurate as we can. To eliminate the job of rewriting, we place the names in random order. When we used to do it alphabetically, a new student meant a new list. Although we may still need to rewrite it, we make sure we have the list of classmates hanging outside the door on the opening day.

It's natural for colleagues to give hints about the children whose names appear on our class lists. "Oh, you probably know who Ralph is. He was in Marsha's class. You know, the one who was always holding her hand so she could keep track of him. And you have Delia. She'll be in the nurse's office more than she's in your classroom. Oh, George. He's really a joy. Wait until you hear him read!" We know our colleagues are trying to help but reality can wait. We have learned not to be flattened or elated by stories about incoming students. There is information about each one that will help as we get to know them but often the quick stories exchanged over the copy machine only fuel the anxiety dreams.

Student Information . . . . First-grade teachers send us articulation forms and attach samples of student writing and a duplicated page of a book at the child's reading level. These two artifacts prove to be most useful as we try to anticipate the range of skills and abilities in the incoming class. We go through these materials with care.

We also read the office files of our new students, including old report cards and registration forms. We collect any information we will need such as birth dates, phone numbers, and parent names to keep handy for future reference.

Checklists . . . . Once the members of the class seem certain, we type the names and draw a grid with five or six boxes after each name. A space at the bottom is designated for the date. Duplicated copies of this list have multiple purposes during the year, from status-of-the-class (Atwell 1987, 73) in writing to keeping track of whose turn it is for the computer. We keep a few of these on a clipboard ready to check off who completed an assignment or who brought in their field trip notices. A stack of them in the file cabinet comes in handy for special teachers, homeroom mothers, and for our continued use during the year. We prefer these typed lists of names to a class record book.

Mailboxes . . . . Students like individual mailboxes. They are a convenient place for them to keep materials that need to go home. We use an old cabinet divided into thirty sections. We put names on each section so they are ready to use on the very first day. Writing these names again helps us to internalize the new class list.

Arranging the Room

When we first enter our classroom in August, it looks like a foreign country. The custodians have moved the furniture to give the room a thorough cleaning. We already know how we want to organize the spaces in the room so it doesn't take us long to make it more familiar. Working on our living space provides a quick and tangible reward as the room shifts back into its familiar setting.

Furniture . . . . We like children to be able to help each other and to work together, so we arrange the desks in groups of four. We can then ask each person to work alone, with a partner, or with a group of four. When the class enrollment is not divisible by four, we add a fifth desk or have a group of two or three. Giving each group a number or name facilitates large group interaction—"Does anyone in group three have another strategy for solving the math challenge?"

We make decisions about other important areas in the room such as the class library, the materials area, and the round tables for small group meetings. We plan several small quiet spaces where two or three children can sit together and collaborate. If we have pillows or beanbag chairs, we decide where they should be. Second graders need to be able to move about the room so we try to provide alternate work sites for those times when students need a change of scene.

Supplies . . . . The independence of our students is a guiding principle in organizing the room. We want to make it possible for them to make decisions while they are working and to get what they need on their own. Workshop times and independent activities flow more smoothly when students know where to find materials, have been taught how to use them, and keep the area tidy. We have different kinds of paper—lined and unlined, large and small—plus recycled notices that still have a clean and blank side to use. The paper is stored on open shelves within student reach. A tray contains a date stamp, staple remover,

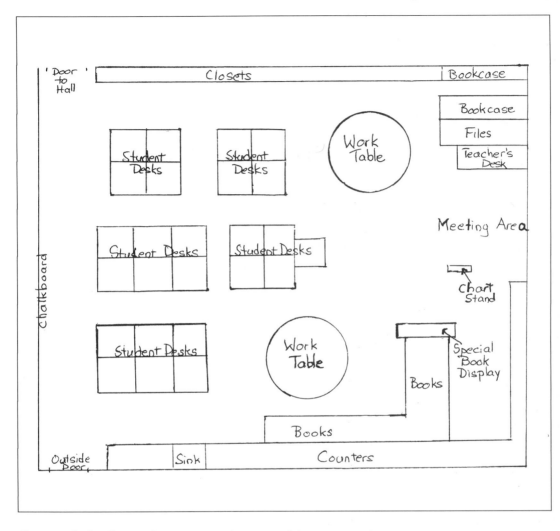

FIGURE 3–1   Room Arrangement (not to scale)

32

staplers, hole punch, markers, colored pencils, and tape. Nearby are glue sticks, scraps of tissue paper and construction paper, scissors, and rulers. According to our state law, the school district must provide its students with school supplies. In August we spend time unpacking and putting away what we ordered in June.

Class Library . . . . We believe that each classroom should have a well-stocked library even if the school library is located next door. There is no substitute for readily available books. We have done this ourselves by collecting books with bonus points from student book orders, by purchasing books, and through using the school and the public libraries to bring a wealth of materials into our rooms. Student-authored books that have been published add to the collection. Donna says in her journal:

> Time to pack up my books to take tomorrow. These are my real friends. I want to see them in the room in the purple bookcase. Then I'll feel ready. At least I haven't had any more anxiety dreams since Friday.

Keeping these books in some semblance of order has been a perennial problem. This fall Donna tried a new way to keep the library organized. Early in the year Donna worked one morning with her students to set up categories, sorting the books into bins. Red was designated for easy readers, purple for author study books, green for poetry, blue for sports, and so on. The students inserted a one-inch-by-eight-inch strip of construction paper in each book according to its category. This has proved to be a workable system for keeping the books organized, but every few weeks the children need to check the bins and rearange where necessary. We continue to pay attention to this kind of organization in order to make it work.

Bulletin Boards . . . . Bulletin boards used to be a September burden. We remember drawing around letters and cutting them out to staple across the top. The first bulletin board, often flashy and eye-catching, demanded several hours to create. We now have a more relaxed and practical attitude. Original student artwork enhances bulletin boards better than any prepackaged product. We cover our bulletin boards with large colored craft paper and leave most of the space available for the children to display their talents. We like to have as much space as possible for our students to create a colorful, pleasing ambience. Reference charts we brainstorm together provide further classroom decoration.

Organizing Support Structures

There are some jobs we can do in August that we know will help prepare us for a calm journey. We want to have information available to everyone in the room and structures in place that will contribute to the smooth functioning of the group.

Schedule of Special Classes . . . . The chunks of time for reading and writing workshops are defined by the schedule of special classes. This schedule is worked out by our principal during the summer and varies from day to day. We print a large chart of when special classes begin and end to ensure that our children arrive at art, the gym, music, the computer lab, and the library at the appointed times. It takes us several weeks to remember library is at 1:30 on Tuesday and the computer lab is at 1:35 on Thursday. As students learn to tell time, they check the schedule and remind us when to go to music.

Daily Schedule . . . . Second graders like to know what happens next. We used to write the schedule for the day on the chalkboard each morning, but then we learned an easier way from a young colleague. We write the activities that will occur during a school day on five-inch-by-eight-inch index cards or strips of colored oak tag. We laminate each card and put a strip of Velcro on the back. We run a self-adhesive strip of Velcro down the chalkboard, making it easy to stick on the schedule each day.

A typical daily schedule may be eight cards hung in a row: reading workshop, snack break, math, writing workshop, lunch and recess, read-aloud time, class meeting, music, and science. We have cards for social studies, field trips, choice time, projects, school program, gym, art, computer lab, the library, and visitors. Students like to arrange the schedule, taking the cards off the Velcro strip and putting up the new ones.

Class Jobs . . . . There are countless ways to organize and display class jobs. Jane uses library pockets and cards with student names in the pockets. The names are rotated weekly. Donna uses a large circle from a pizza box to list the jobs and clothespins with the name of each child that rotate one space around the circle each week. Regardless of how the jobs are displayed, we agree that everyone in the room has a job each week. Job needs change from year to year and larger classes may mean that some jobs are assigned to two children. Here is a list we consider:

- attendance: taking the roll to the office;
- lunch: counting and entering orders and taking orders to cafeteria;
- plants: watering as needed;
- calendar: placing numerals on calendar and saying the date;
- line leader: first in line;
- door holder: second in line;
- notices: placing in mailboxes;
- closet doors: keeping them closed;
- librarian: keeping book collection orderly;
- chalkboard: erasing and washing;
- floor: picking up litter;
- manipulatives: distributing and putting away math and science materials;
- windows: opening and closing as needed;
- messenger: delivering notes, books, and so on;
- hospitality: guiding a visitor in classroom;
- lights: saving electricity whenever possible;
- computer: turning off, organizing disks;
- listening center: turning the tape recorder off and putting tapes away;
- games: puting away and organizing;
- playground equipment: caring for;
- job chart: changing weekly;
- flag salute: leading;
- math center: organizing materials;
- paper/folders: distributing and collecting;
- daily schedule: changing the signs; and
- vacation: filling in for an absentee.

Students suggest jobs that are needed for a smoother flow. One year in Jane's class, Andrew suggested that someone write the numbers of the buses as they were announced on the intercom at dismissal time. This idea helped everyone remain calm during a hectic time. When Donna's class adopted a gerbil, taking care of Lucky was added to the job chart.

Attendance and Lunch Count . . . . We try to structure the morning to minimize the time spent on school-mandated noninstructional tasks such as taking the attendance and lunch orders. Donna has a large chart with the name of each student listed. When students enter the room in the morning, they take a clothespin with their name on it off the name chart and move it to the large chart that lists choices for lunch. It takes but a few seconds to note who is absent and to jot down what children want to order for lunch. This process becomes a student job later in the year. In Jane's class a student writes the next morning's choices on the board at dismissal. Children tally their lunch choice when they enter the room each morning. She can see at a glance who is not sitting at their desk for the attendance. Whatever the method, the first few weeks of school we take time to help children develop the pattern that gives us the information we need. These rituals mean that time spent together at the beginning of a day can be more meaningful than "Who is ordering hot dogs?"

Bathroom and Library . . . . On the chalkboard near the door to the hallway we have a small space for children to sign out when they wish to go to the bathroom. They do not need to ask but must observe the rule that only one person at a time may go to each bathroom. Of course, we make exceptions for emergencies. There is also a place to sign out for the library. A quick look at the board tells us where students are. Students value this extra degree of independence.

Organizing and Making Materials

There are some things we know we will need the first few days and having them ready helps us concentrate on our most important role, that of learning to know and understand a new group of students. We prepare these materials in August in the quiet of an empty classroom.

Books for Writing Workshop . . . . Second graders find it special to write in already prepared books; flat paper doesn't hold the same allure. We begin writing workshop on the first day of school so we get a number of blank books ready. This year a former student helped Jane make three different kinds of books: one had three sheets of plain white paper folded and stapled together, a second had a cover of plain blue paper with lined pages, and the third had a yellow cover with a picture space at the top of the page and lines on the bottom. These books are stored with the other paper so children can choose the kind that will best suit their writing. Coding the covers with colored duplicating paper makes it easier for students to choose the kind of blank book they want.

Graphs . . . . In the beginning of the year graphs help us get to know each other better. We reduce stress for ourselves by making these large charts ahead of time, adding appropriate titles and details as we use them. On a busy morning when there is no time to get out the yardstick and markers, it is a comfort to pull out a graph all ready to roll. We try to have five or six such graphs prepared.

Some graphs are factual, like birth month and position in the family. Others are designed to get children to think about some of their personal choices. The morning message asks students to add their name to a graph before the day begins. Later in the day, we give students time to jot down something they have learned about the class from the graph. Then the class shares information. Graph topics that second graders enjoy are:

- birthdays;
- birth order among siblings;
- whether they are six, seven, or eight years old;
- a favorite color;
- a pet graph introducing the use of a Venn diagram, as some children have both cats and dogs;
- the number of pockets being worn by each person today, repeated for a week;
- favorite seasons of the year;
- favorite subjects in school;
- where they like to read—in a cozy corner or at their desk; and
- whether they prefer to be read to or to read on their own.

As we discuss the results, we discover interesting information about each other. We hang the graphs in the hall or around the room so parents can learn about the class when they come for back-to-school night. Next to each one we write a brief list of facts the children have observed. For example, this year we learned that eleven children in the class are the youngest in their family, no one is an only child, four are in the middle, and ten children are the oldest.

If we don't want to keep the results, we draw a graph on the chalkboard and children add their names on stick-ems or write on the board, which Jane found made doing a daily graph easy. After having some experiences with graphs during the first few weeks of school, children begin suggesting topics. When students were choosing chocolate or vanilla cupcakes for Sophie's birthday celebration, she suggested a topic: Do you prefer chocolate or vanilla cupcakes? One day in October, Liz taped a Halloween drawing to the side of her desk. A paper stapled to the bottom said, Do you like my drawing? She had a column for yes and another for no.

Papers for Reading and Writing . . . . We have special papers we like to use for certain activities such as reading responses, writing Weekend News, and Room 13 News. We prepare these sheets, make revisions to old ones as needed, and duplicate them so that they are ready when school begins. These papers are placed in special baskets in a convenient place on the windowsill so that children know where to find them. We will describe how we use them in Chapters 4 and 5.

Materials for the First Day . . . . Before we can take a deep breath and feel ready for the first day, we need to be sure we have the materials we will need at our fingertips. Pencils need points, colored folders for reading and writing workshop are counted and stacked, and duplicated copies of special activities are run on the copy machine and organized. Oak-tag strips are cut for name tags. An attendance slip is ready. Calendar numbers are in their proper place. Read-aloud materials are selected and a morning message is written on the board.

The name tags will be made by each child to put on desks. Donna used to make name tags as one of the jobs she did to get ready for school, but Jane convinced her that second graders prefer to write their own names and are capable of doing a splendid job. They like to decorate these name tags before we laminate them later that first week of school and tape them to their desks.

We have made our preparations sound smooth and flawless, but these tasks are accomplished amid many interruptions. Old friends, colleagues, students, and parents drop by to exchange summer stories. New students and parents come to meet us. Other professionals in the building stop by with vital information about incoming students. Our preparations are done as we juggle our needs with social and professional interludes. If we have somehow managed to tend to our long list of tasks, and if the planets are in the right orbit, we leave our room before the big day with anticipation and excitement.

Not all beginnings are as carefully orchestrated as we would wish. This fall a friend had a family emergency the week before school started. As she left the building the night before opening day, she backed her station wagon up to the door of her room and loaded it with extraneous materials that still needed to be sorted and put away. The next morning her room looked organized and ready. She emptied the back of her car after school and put everything away. There are times when we improvise and the appearance of readiness is the best we can do.

Even though our preparations seem unforgettable, we cannot

always remember from year to year exactly what we did and what worked well. Since we became teacher-researchers, we have been in the habit of jotting down what happens in our classrooms. It helps to look back and be reminded of what needs to be done that might not be obvious. We keep some notes about August activities. Although the following fall may seem light years away, we are grateful for our own guidance when we are ready to begin again.

We want the beginning of the school year to be as organized, upbeat, and enjoyable for our students as we can possibly make it. We want to be clearheaded so we can deal with the unexpected and appear unhassled no matter how excited we feel inside. Here's another entry from Donna's journal:

> School starts tomorrow. I'm ready. I'm so ready I'm well past ripe. I'd fall off the tree if I were an apple. I've typed up a list of twenty things to do tomorrow. No doubt that's overkill, but nothing would terrify me more than having twenty kids staring at me and nothing to do. Now the real test, to see if I can fall asleep. My body is beat but my mind is racing. It doesn't help that there is a full moon.

Classroom Structures and Rituals

The first day of school marks another milestone. Children are often referred to by their grade. To become a second grader is to achieve a new status. Stephanie was ready to forsake the beach long before the date rolled around on the calendar. Many children are, although they may worry whether their new label will fit comfortably and how they will do in this new phase of their lives. Our goals for these first days are twofold: We want to begin building relationships with and among our students that will allow all of us to stretch and succeed during the year. We also want to put in place some of the rituals and patterns that will guide us for the year, which is why we fuss like a mother of the bride to get all the details in place before the music starts.

What we do the first day of school may leave an indelible mark on the group and we want that mark to be positive. Children come through the door filled with trepidation and hope. We want them to go home that first afternoon anticipating their best year ever. On the evening of the first day of first grade, Donna's son Scott wrote this message on the chalkboard in his bedroom: "Mi mom iz the skond best prsn in the wrld." Donna hugged him as she counted her blessings. Scott would have a good first-grade year; his teacher, Mrs. Sue, had already won his heart.

With our sky-high goals in mind, we plan those first hours together so they will be productive for students and begin to shape the structures and rituals that will support our learning community for the next ten months.

Morning Messages and Responsibilities
When all the children are accounted for, we begin our first day together. Many have read the morning message on the board. A fresh one will greet them each day, an idea we got from Wendy Wu, a Westport colleague, when she first began teaching in our district. The message tells them of any special events and what they should work on. The first morning message might read like this:

> Welcome to second grade! I hope you had a wonderful summer. I did. Please print your name in large letters on the oak tag. Decorate it for your desk.
> We will have a great year.
>
> *Mrs. Skolnick*

As the message is read aloud each morning it becomes part of our reading instruction done in the context of a daily routine. The following are some instructional springboards we may use with the morning message:

- patterns in the language of the message to familiarize students with new words and give them repeated practice;
- new vocabulary, plurals, or contractions;
- vowel patterns if a group of children needs that practice;
- deliberate mistakes in spelling or punctuation;
- spaces left blank, leading to a discussion of appropriate words for the empty place and the use of contextual clues; and
- punctuation omitted and then inserted by the group.

Morning rituals set the tone for the day. We want children to be able to walk into the room and know what lies ahead. The predictable pattern of the early morning eases the transition between home and school. For seven- and eight-year-olds, the stability of a consistent start fits their developmental needs.

Children quickly learn the morning pattern: hang backpacks in closet, put notes from home into the labeled basket, move clothespin for lunch count or tally on the board, read the morning message, and settle into what needs to be done. Once we start the day, they can count on a short meeting to discuss the day ahead, the reading of the morning message together, a talk about the calendar, and any assigned work. Then we move to the meeting area on the rug to listen to a good book.

There are endless ways to start the day and we have experimented with many variations through the years. Some classes listen best if we begin in the meeting area. Others prefer to be at their desks for the first ten minutes of school business. Whatever ritual we establish, we try to have it match the needs of the children and become a pattern that feels right as we repeat it day after day.

When we meet to share the favorite book they brought that first morning, we establish another important routine. As each child shares, we emphasize the importance of listening attentively to each other. We encourage them to address what they say to the group, not just to the teacher. As they return to their seats to read quietly, we also read to model our own pleasure in reading and then circulate, bending down at desks, to chat briefly with readers about their books. We reinforce our belief that books make the world a better place.

Transition Times

Moving from one activity to another can be the bane of a teacher's existence unless time is taken to set a tone for these moments. We make it clear that we expect everyone to move to and from the meeting place smoothly, but we are not drill sergeants. It takes some children longer than others. We know Jesse may be bursting to say something to Stephen, his best friend, and that he needs to take this opportunity to do so.

We request that everyone come with whatever materials they need for the next activity in the circle as quickly and quietly as they can. If a straggler is left behind, the pressure of the rest of the group beginning a new activity encourages that child to join. When important things are happening no one wants to be left out. If we have a class of twenty-five we may make more of a ceremony in order to get everyone moved without mishaps. We may establish a pattern: stand up, push in your chair, stand behind it. Table three may join us in the meeting place.

We also establish patterns for getting ready to go to gym. Those who need to change to sneakers do so quickly as we call tables or individuals to get in line. If the room is very noisy, asking only Amy and Brian to line up sends a message that spreads like wildfire. Everyone becomes quiet because they are anxious to get in line.

There are patterns for getting ready for lunch, which include washing hands. Those who need to go to the bathroom sign up on the chalkboard and learn to take turns without needing our attention. They wash in the bathroom. Others wash at the sink in the classroom. We ask them to do this in small groups, usually one table at a time.

An orderly dismissal time at the end of the day is something we work to achieve anew each year. We ask children to get ready by tables, empty their mailboxes, get their backpacks and outdoor clothing, and sit quietly in the meeting place. We may rehearse students to share what has happened in school with adults at home, taking a few extra minutes for this activity. We pose a central question such as, "What did you learn in your reading response group today?" Each child takes a turn, following the rule that no one repeats what someone else has said, although piggybacking on someone's idea is fine. Other times we may recite poems we have learned.

Because we have everyone ready and quiet in the circle, as the school secretary begins to announce the buses on the loudspeaker, children get up to leave quietly, shake our hand good-bye, listen to a personal comment, and walk down the hall. The other students remain in the meeting place until their buses are announced.

What we are describing is the ideal we have occasionally reached, but dismissal time is difficult for young children. They are anxious about the possibility of missing their buses and anxious to get on with the next part of their day. Achieving a moderate decorum at this time is often the best we can hope for. Jane's personal journal notes her strong feelings about the end of the school day:

> Dismissal is when everything seems to break into individual pieces, each child turned inward and thinking of himself alone. Everyone is tired and ready for a change. We may have had a great sense of the group with respect and helpfulness during the day, but that can disappear instantly when the first parent appears to pick up a child or the first bus is called on the intercom from the office. Sometimes teachers say they think our school day is too long, but dismissal time is the same whether the day is long or short. A different time for leaving each other would not affect the almost animal-like feelings that seem to burst forth. Good routines, consistent enforcement of rules and expectations are essential but, try as I may, I have not solved this puzzle.

We stay with our students until they have all left the room, saying good-bye to each person individually. We need to get ready for our after-school work. Some afternoons we have meetings. Other afternoons we stay in the classroom. We look at the work that has been done that day, think about individual children and their needs, prepare for the next day, and write observations in our journals. We usually take work with us to do at home.

Completion of Work

On day one we begin to set in place the patterns of behavior we expect of our students when a task is completed. Helping seven- and eight-year-olds become independent is important because it helps us to work without interruptions. Our goal is to have everyone purposefully occupied with a job that is important.

We set up baskets that are clearly marked and in a convenient place where children can place their work when it is finished. We want to be sure the work is not placed in mailboxes or lost in desks until we have seen it. We use one of our checklists to make sure students have carried out their responsibilities as we look over the material in the basket.

We begin to develop a repertoire of possible activities for children when they have completed writing Weekend News or a reading response. This list appears on a reference chart in the classroom so students can use it to help decide when they are looking for a new activity. We discuss these alternatives at the end of Chapter 4.

Classroom Issues

Social threads run through the tapestry of every classroom, but seven- and eight-year-olds put their own special twist on these threads. We expect to spend time in September on interpersonal issues. The quality of life in the room improves as we help children learn to interact in kind and thoughtful ways. The investment in time is worthwhile as it gives children the strong message that we have definite expectations about how they should treat each other.

Where we give our attention is crucial to the group. A delicate balance must be found between what to focus on and what to ignore. Some things escalate beyond reasonable bounds if not dealt with immediately. Others can be quietly overlooked and will disappear without a trace. We try to put a positive slant on any issue we decide to deal with. Waiting for squirmy bodies to settle in after recess, Donna might say, "Raise your hand if you are sitting quietly and are ready to listen."

Conflict Resolution

Conflicts and disagreements are bound to arise as the class begins to get better acquainted. Position in line may seem inordinately important.

"He cut me," said Randy, genuinely offended. "I did *not*," said Jim, "Albert was saving this place for me." One second grader can shrug his shoulders when someone crowds ahead in line on the way to gym. But to the child who values fairness highly, this may be a capital offense.

Another issue that can undo some seven year olds is lost property. When Gabrielle had a shiny pencil just like the one Meredith lost, it was difficult for Meredith not to demand her pencil back.

A third predictable type of problem is unkindness. Seven- and eight-year-olds are trying out different behaviors. Some may have a low tolerance for frustration or minimal impulse control. They may be reflecting tensions in school or at home, something they watched on television, or emulating heroes among older children.

Whatever the source of tension, we have found several ways to help ease relationships in the crowded space we share.

Deciding on Explicit Rules . . . . We create the classroom rules with our students. When children help to write and then sign the list of class rules that hangs in the room, a sense of authorship promotes greater cooperation. The time spent discussing rules and making sure we all agree on language and meaning paves the way for fewer disputes later on.

The group has a solid foundation of acceptable and expected behavior when rules are decided by consensus and displayed publicly. Donna's class agreed on general rules the first week of school. During class meetings once a week in September, they discussed and decided other important class issues—how to share personal items such as markers and the consequences for breaking rules. Because fairness is such a central concern at this age, these rules are printed on large chart paper and hung on the wall.

Role-Playing Potential Problems . . . . There are predictable peer problems in second grade. Role-playing is an active and informative way to help children know what to say and how to respond verbally. Children can role-play how to walk in line and how *not* to walk in line. They enjoy seeing their teacher do it the wrong way, crowding the person ahead or draping arms over shoulders. Children this age need help learning how to handle someone who is unkind. We have children role-play what to do or say if someone says something mean. A quick remark tossed out can reduce another to tears. Rachel cried when Jennifer told her "You're stupid." Role-playing what to say to Jennifer helped her deal with her feelings as she practiced how to handle a difficult situation.

Talking It Over . . . . We handle personal conflicts as soon as we can. As children begin to trust that we will not ignore their problems, they become willing to wait for an appropriate time to discuss a particular problem. Most children this age are able to take turns in explaining differing views of a controversy. We give each person an opportunity to explain the conflicting points of view.

We encourage students to arrive at their own solution. When that is not possible, we assume the role of arbiter. Two earnest and honest students, Margaret and Amy, both laid claim to the same small eraser shaped like a watermelon. They needed Jane to help. She asked them to put the eraser on her desk overnight until a decision could be reached. In the freshness of the morning, the eraser lost its value and Margaret willingly agreed to accept a brand-new pink school eraser.

As students learn to listen to each other during a dispute, we ask them to step into the hall to talk and try to reach a solution. It is gratifying when they reenter the room as friends. Perhaps the privacy of the hall or the time alone allows them to calm down and reach agreement.

Ashley and Tanya were having a bad day together. Normally they were very good friends, but something happened on the playground and Ashley came into the room convinced that she was never going to speak with Tanya again. She was very upset. Jane asked them to go out in the hall and try to talk it over. They stayed and stayed. The rest of the class resumed normal activities. Suddenly the door burst open and loud giggles could be heard. Ashley and Tanya entered the room, arms around each other. Everyone was astonished, not knowing how this had happened but delighted to see them so happy.

We try to model and encourage thoughtful behavior and hope that with continued practice and awareness, our students will grow in their ability to resolve conflicts. We want our students to know, however, that we are always there when they need us.

Getting Their Attention

Another decision that has to be made each fall is how we choose to get the attention of the class. The old standby—talking louder than they do—takes a lot of energy and doesn't feel right. We prefer our classrooms to have a quiet hum, realizing that the louder our talking voice, the louder the volume of every voice. The signal for attention and quiet needs to be explained and practiced.

Donna prefers to ring a bell. Jane may stop, ask for their attention, and simply wait. Or we may shut off the overhead lights. We explain our signals to the students and ask them to practice responding to it. Once a signal is given we wait patiently until we have the complete attention of the group. We have seen teachers raise a hand and have each child stop and do the same. Some teachers clap a short pattern that the children clap back. Kate Sanderson, a first-grade teacher in our building, softly plays a triangle.

Once we have their attention, we phrase our message carefully. We want our requests to be positive. We state precisely what we want done in a quiet voice—"Please walk in the hall," not "Don't run." Students learn that we do not repeat general information and what we say will be succinct.

One year Donna's class loved the tape of Kermit the Frog singing "The Rainbow Connection." When it was time to clean up, Donna played the tape. It was a signal to get busy putting away materials and clearing off desks. It was fun to do it with a favorite song playing in the background.

Pacing

When we return to school in the fall we may still be in the rhythm of the previous June. We need to continually remind ourselves that it is September and that our students are really tall first graders. We may get in sync with their slower pace by Friday of the first week but lose it over the weekend. We have to work to get back to the early second-grade rhythm on Monday. Donna confides to her journal:

> This week I feel like I'm getting my voice as a teacher. Am I Miss Nelson or Viola Swamp? Am I a nag or someone who chooses to ignore a lot of kid behavior if it doesn't cross the line? Where is the line? Monday I felt like I was in a large, round raft with the kids and there were twenty-one paddles in the water. The challenge was to get into the current where we could move in a good direction together. It felt like we were making progress by the end of the week. I also realized that I like spending my day with these kids. I'm totally absorbed in what I'm doing. There's never a minute when I'm bored or wondering what I should be doing or thinking something other than what's happening right in that moment.

Another entry a week later reads:

So much has happened in the last week that I don't want to forget. There was an hour or so last Monday when everything seemed impossible and I thought maybe I'd just go to the parking lot, get in the car, and drive away. The kids seemed so restless, unable to listen or follow directions. But probably part of it was my own impatience with their rhythm and speed. And, of course, they all have different rhythms and speeds.

Beginning second graders need a rhythm that responds to their need to move and change activities with a fair amount of frequency. Squirmy bodies or distracted stares signal the time to wrap it up and move along.

The first few weeks were so hard because my pace was all wrong. What I'd plan to do in one day would take one week. I tried making lesson plans the way I did fifteen years ago and I ended up fragmenting the day and trying to rush the kids to finish something (anything). My wonderful supportive colleagues counsel me that the first month is establishing the group, etc., and that I should be patient. So I'm revising every day, yet trying to be consistent, and there is a glimmer of light at the end of the tunnel.

The pace changes significantly as the year progresses, but early in the year short and sweet is in order. We aim for a healthy variety of activities to capture the attention and interest of each learner in the room.

To someone fresh from the adult world of sabbatical, our pace matched the snail's in the classroom terrarium. I started the year planning our activities by the clock, rather than by the interests and needs of the children—a sure-fire way to frustrate all of us. Planning each lesson and the day the way I had fifteen years ago denied the shift in my own teaching pedagogy. I could no longer teach page fifty-three on Tuesday because I had taught page fifty-two on Monday. By October I had abandoned my large, black lesson plan book for a spiral notebook. Journal entries and plans share the pages and allow for the flexible, response-based teaching that serves the students and my own concept of how children learn.

Helping Us Know Each Other

Building a community within our classroom is more than what happens during reading and writing workshop. Many things contribute to our sense of community, including regular class meetings, doing cooperative work, small blocks of time when children are having snacks or getting ready for lunch, and the physical arrangement of the room.

Letter to Parents

At the end of the first week, we send home a letter to parents. The introductory text contains some general words about the beginning of school and the pleasure of working with this group of children. We ask parents to help us "know your child better by answering the three questions" contained in the letter and returning their answers to school the following week. Leaving perhaps a half-page of space for each question, we ask,

1. What would you like me to know about your child?
2. How does your child spend time on his/her own at home?
3. What are your goals/expectations for your child this year?

Most parents take the time to answer our questions and their answers are very thoughtful, sometimes even poignant. Matthew's mother wrote,

> I've always felt that one of his greatest strengths was his social skill for leading other children, making friends, and adapting to any new situation. He acts very mature and self-sufficient for his age and I sometimes forget that he's only seven and a half and needs a more loving or softer, more patient approach. However, he definitely seems to have some insecurities about his academic abilities, particularly since he repeated first grade. I'd love to see him feel free to experiment and be wrong.

Kate's mother wrote,

> When it comes to actually sitting down and focusing on something that may not come easy to her, I think she does anything she can to dance around it. Therefore, gentle, but firm direction is necessary.

Sara's mother wrote,

> Sara is an only child and her father and I are going

through a divorce. She hides her feelings about most things. She is very sensitive, she is the peacemaker if someone is upset or hurt. . . . I want her to have a very good self-image.

Jamie's mother wrote,

Jamie likes to be funny—always doing silly things to make people laugh. We sometimes fear this is a mechanism to cover some feelings of inadequacy. . . . He is the middle child in our family and probably hasn't had so much "one-on-one" attention as he would have liked.

Life Boxes

Life boxes help students to get to know each other better. Donna introduces them by reading *Wilfred Gordon McDonald Partridge* (Fox 1985). In that tender picture book, a small boy gathers a collection of his things to help Miss Nancy get back her lost memory. Donna shares her life box, explaining the significance of her polished cube inscribed with "Writer's Block," the picture of her children playing among wildflowers in Wyoming, her Playbill from *Phantom of the Opera*, and her *Book Lover's Journal*. She invites the children to collect five things that matter to them to share with the group.

Over the next few days the room fills with individual treasures as the children bring in their life boxes to share. As the class sits in a circle and listens to each child describe their important objects, they add to their knowledge of each other. Pearson brought in a bag of crystal and amethyst quartz, a picture of himself in his dad's mailbox, and a soccer trophy. Michele shared some long yarn she had woven together, pencils to show she likes to write, and a small glass animal like the ones she collects. The contents of life boxes also provide ideas for stories during writing workshop. Some teachers have found ways to incorporate their contents into math, such as using them for graphs or probability exercises.

Changing Seats Often

Our seating arrangement in groups of four allows children to get to know each other. We change seats every three or four weeks by having students draw from a selected and shuffled deck of cards with four aces for group one, four twos for group two, and so on. Jane prefers children to empty their desks and move their belongings to a new seat. Donna finds students become attached to their desks and her students slide their desks to a new location.

If a special-needs child must be in a certain place in order to hear or to focus better, we give that child a card before the rest of the children draw. Students know these seats are for a short period of time, but if someone finds a seat particularly difficult, we may make an adjustment. Changing seats broadens the friendships and respect in the class. Alison looked disappointed when she ended up with three boys. But in a day or so, Jane noticed that she was enjoying her new group and the boys were developing a respect for Alison as they included her in the decisions the group made.

Informal Moments

Seven- and eight-year-olds need time to work and play together. The fifteen minutes before school when the buses are arriving is a time students can chat together as they begin the work assigned in the morning message. This informal time gives them a chance to tell about the new cousin who was born or the white-tailed deer they saw in the backyard. The better children get to know each other, the more they shift these conversations from us to their peers. We know we are doing our job as children seek out each other to share news.

Another more relaxed time is when students are getting ready for lunch. We overhear interesting conversations that may or may not be related to school work. These are important times if we are to keep school humane and build a close community.

Choice Time

Once a week we schedule a time when children can make choices about what to do. Choice time is an unstructured twenty or thirty minutes when students may read, write, build with blocks, use the computer, play checkers, or perform a play. They are only limited by their imagination. Some students plan ahead and bring activities from home. Kristin taught a group of girls how to braid lanyards. Ashley brought embroidery thread to make bracelets. Boys often use this time to examine baseball cards or draw mazes or cartoons. So that all members of the class may enjoy what they are doing without a sense of chaos, we request quiet voices. A three-bell limit reminds everyone to regulate the decibels. The first two bells warn that the noise level is too high. The third bell means it is time to put everything away early. We rarely get to the third bell, but students know we will follow through if it happens and this rule puts the ball in their court. Sometimes an overzealous group playing with Marble Works needs a quiet reminder, but we know children this age can comply with rules and still enjoy themselves with friends.

Snack Break

When the weather is too cold or wet to go outside for a morning snack and recess, we set aside fifteen minutes in the room to pursue activities of individual choice. This is another fertile time for new friendships. At the end of September, Donna asked her class to fill out a questionnaire about the year so far. Walt, who was new to the school and still mourned the move from Texas, wrote a one-word answer in capital letters: "FRIENDS!" We celebrated his response. Having a friend can change a gray sky to blue.

Working with Friends

We arrange our reading program early in the year to provide opportunities for children to read with partners and in small groups. The relaxed conversations sparked by a good story and a growing sense of power about reading can lead to deeper relationships. Conversations about writing help new friends gain respect for each other as they become better acquainted.

We work best in a classroom where the dominant feeling is one of calm, purposeful, and quiet conversations so we help students understand the reason behind their need to use a "tell-a-secret" voice. We can allow for conversations and relationship building during most independent work times. On the questionnaire referred to earlier, Donna asked students about their preferred working environment.

I do my best work: in a silent room
                    when we use quiet voices
                    when the room is noisy

Only one child checked the last response. When the request for quiet voices is not a teacher demand but an agreed-on condition by the class, commitment increases. There are some children who work best in a quiet setting. We provide time for both silent reading and silent writing. There are also spaces in the room and in the hall sheltered from most sounds.

We plan other activities that involve students working together. On one of the first days of school we play people bingo. Each child has a grid of twenty spaces arranged in rows of four or five. Children move around the room, filling each space with the signature of a classmate. After this has been done, a child draws the names one at a time, reading them aloud. Children cover those names on their game board with counters, playing bingo in the traditional way. We may also use a graphing activity to help children become better acquainted. Alex asked: Have you ever moved? Mindy asked: Do you have a dog?

We encourage students to use each other's names as much as possible. Jane teaches her class the name game on the first morning, when they meet in a circle. Courtney is sitting on Jane's right. Next to Courtney is Rachel. Jane starts: "This is Courtney and my name is Mrs. Fraser." Courtney then says, "This is Rachel and I am Courtney," and so on around the circle. Later, it is fun to introduce three people at a time, or the positions in the circle can be mixed up and the game played again.

We try not to make assumptions about the social skills of seven-year-olds. Like other skills, the range of social abilities varies widely. All children can learn from role-playing, modeling, and taking time to talk about how to be a friend or a working partner. We do not take it for granted that young children can get along with each other as a natural happening.

> Today felt the best so far. I didn't have to work so hard to get through the day. The three days last week were adventurous and new, but the rhythm seemed uneven and I went from one activity to another without a sense of flow. Besides, all the activities I carefully planned for Wednesday took us until Friday to get through, and there are still some I decided to bag for the time being. I have so much to learn about these kids.

Each school year is a new beginning. There are certain patterns we can use from previous years, but the orchestra will play a new song depending upon the character of its members, current events, family constellations, and the air pressure. The surprises in this new melody keep teaching young children exciting. We would not want it to be a repetition of the year before or the year before that.

Getting ready and putting in place certain patterns and structures helps us to conduct the orchestra to play a full, rich sound. After being the leader for a while, we can step aside and let others share the lead. This is when we know we are doing a good job—we are transferring some of the direction to younger members of our community as it begins to harmonize.

References

Atwell, Nancie. 1987. *In the Middle: Writing, Reading, and Learning with Adolescents*. Portsmouth, NH: Boynton/Cook.

Fox, Mem. 1985. *Wilfred Gordon McDonald Partridge*. Brooklyn, NY: Kane/Miller.

Pass the Book: Reading with Second Graders

4

❧ Nicky was a bright boy who loved to draw. It seemed as though he put no effort into reading. He would stare into space wrapped in his own dreams. One morning he arrived very excited, thrusting forward a copy of the Eyewitness Jr. book *Amazing Snakes* (Parsons 1990), which his father had brought home from a business trip. This book transformed Nicky as he poured over the pages, reading and considering the artwork. The daydreamer had become hooked on a book.

Our comprehensive literature-based reading program has evolved over the years and stems from our philosophy of how children grow as readers, writers, and learners. This program contains ten strands that fit together to shape a second-grade year with a variety of enjoyable and engaging activities appropriate for this age group.

We looked at these strands and identified ten strategic practices we use when teaching reading. For purposes of organization, we made a chart that shows one strategic practice for each reading strand. These practices are really used throughout the teaching day in everything we do. We have chosen to highlight one in each section, but we ask you to imagine each one as a different color creating a rainbow of strategic practices arching through each strand. Like Legos, they fit together to support all the different aspects of our reading program and the learning environment in our classrooms.

Whatever work is being done in the reading classroom, we structure the routine to facilitate work that is productive and satisfying. Students work together as a class, in smaller groups, with partners, and as individuals. With appropriate routines and patterns in place, we can

STRATEGIC PRACTICES	READING STRANDS
Encouragement of thoughtfulness	Response to literature
Choice, flexibility	Author Studies
Integration of Curriculum	Text sets
Fostering individual pursuit Focus on strengths	Nonfiction
Teaching skills in context	Whole Class Novel
Authenticity, Modeling	Independent Reading
Immersion in language	Reading Aloud
Making criteria explicit	Reference Charts
Connected teaching	Poetry
Shared decision-making	Readers' Theater, Drama

This chart shows the strategic practices we use in our teaching. We have chosen to explain each practice in terms of a reading strand that illustrates it especially well, but it is not exclusive to that strand. For example, cooperation might also be listed in response to literature, author studies, text sets, nonfiction, whole class novel, and poetry. These practices are also found in our writing **workshop and throughout the day. (See chapters four through eight.)**

FIGURE 4–1 Strategic Practices

move among our students, encouraging, nudging, teaching, confirming, appreciating, and celebrating their work.

We view reading as a collaborative effort among all the learners. Our days are filled with surprises. The goal we keep in mind is to assist students in becoming joyfully literate, not to teach books or specific content. We want to pass along the pleasure and knowledge we gain from our own passion for reading and writing. We may be the oldest and the tallest learners, but we know that second graders have their own important thoughts. Utilizing all the thinking in the room casts a brighter, more clarifying light upon our reading path.

The children who enter our classes have a wide range of abilities, from avid and experienced readers to reluctant ones. In September Kat was a solid fourth-grade reader. She had read over one hundred novels during the summer. Adrienne was still struggling with basic word patterns. The other six-, seven-, and eight-year-olds ran the gamut from dependent and unsure to independent and competent.

They had one quality in common: they loved to listen to stories. The first morning when Donna read *Teacher From the Black Lagoon* (Thaler 1989), their upturned faces were spellbound. A smile spread across David's face when the creature-teacher scraped her claws down the chalkboard. After recess they listened attentively to the first chapter in *My Father's Dragon* (Gannett 1987) and eagerly voted to hear the second chapter. Working with these young readers promised to be rewarding. They happily surrendered to the power of a well-told tale. With our rooms full of books, we have what we need to help them on their way to full-fledged membership in the literacy club.

Response to Literature
Responding to literature is a natural part of our reading routine. As students discuss the books we read aloud, their oral responses transfer individual ideas into the collective realm and are a rehearsal for thinking on paper. Written responses parallel oral responses but become more personal. Students also respond in project form by making puppets, posters, mobiles, or murals. Students know that their opinions and ideas about literature are valued

The pulse of our reading program is how we listen to students and take cues from them. We see more in our students than they see in themselves and we are curious to know their thinking as they latch onto interpretations different from our own. One of the pleasures of our day is to glimpse the world through their eyes as they connect a book to their own life events.

Oral Responses

Reading a picture book aloud is a relaxing way to ease into the day. After the class reads the morning message and takes care of school business, we meet on the rug in the back of the room and anticipate the pleasure of a good story. We can almost feel the way it wraps a web of words and wonder around us and invites us back into our literary group after a night of separation. We choose the picture books carefully. We want the words of the text to enchant us and the illustrations to capture our imaginations. The richer the text, the richer and more dynamic the discussion that follows.

We think of our discussions as conversations among readers. We delight as we hear the voices of our students become more confident. The conversation becomes more meaningful when seven- and eight-year-olds listen to each other and piggyback ideas. Jane recorded this dialogue in her journal:

JAMIE: I was reading *Henry and Mudge in Puddle Trouble* [Rylant 1990b]. It reminded me of the time I got in trouble. I came in the house soaking wet because I ran through a puddle.

MELISSA: That happened to me. My mom was furious.

TIM: Henry and Mudge are so neat. They always do things like we do. The author must have a kid our age.

"Pass the book" is a quick, purposeful oral sharing. After reading *Spinky Sulks* (Steig 1988) to entranced students, Jane could see the book had sparked many ideas. She passed the book to Alex, who was sitting next to her in the circle, saying, "Tell what you noticed about the book and pass it along. Please don't repeat what has already been said."

Alex smiled as he hugged the book. "I think Spinky is a spoiled brat just liked my brother Evan." Laughter and nods of agreement moved around the circle. He passed the book to Casey, who said, "I liked when Spinky dressed like a clown and made the party for his family. Sometimes he could be nice." He handed the book to Arielle, who said, "This is the first William Steig book we've read with people. He usually uses animals for characters, like Solomon and Sylvester."

The book traveled around the circle, creating a magical force field that riveted the attention on each speaker. Children at the end of the circle only had to flip through the pages to come up with a fresh idea. They surprised themselves with how many relevant and interesting comments they could make. Not all books are as provocative as *Spinky Sulks,* but we can sense when everyone wants to talk about a story. "Pass the book" gives everyone a chance to share observations. With the actual book in hand, a student digs deeper for what to say. Children who wish may always do what we do with the book and pass.

Anne Nesbitt, who also teaches second grade in our school, devised a quick way to hear all the voices in the room as she gently pulls the gathering thread at the end of silent reading. When the timer rings, students tell where they were during the last fifteen minutes. The first time we asked there were puzzled looks.

"I spent the last half hour in London," Donna told them.

"I was right here, by the bookcase," Bryan proclaimed.

Ashley came to the rescue. "Oh, I get it," she said. "I was reading *Charlotte's Web* [White 1952]. I was at the county fair."

Jordan's hand shot into the air. "I was reading *Herbie Jones and the Dark Attic* [Kline 1992]. I was up in a spooky attic."

More hands flew up. Donna started listing the places the class had been. Excitement mounted as readers eagerly told where their books had taken them. The books had transported them beyond the walls of room 14. They had been on a mountain, under the ocean, in outer space, and visiting another school. The children celebrated the power of books and their growing ability to travel between the printed page and imaginary worlds.

We may end a reading period by asking who they were with as they read. Second graders find it amusing to report that they were with a mouse riding a motorcycle or with a dinosaur that was lost or with Adam Joshua and his dog George (Smith 1988). "Aren't we lucky?" Sophie declared once in a burst of enthusiasm. "We met new friends and we never left the room!"

Written Responses

Our postcard to students in August welcomes them to second grade and invites them to bring their favorite book the first day of school. When they crowd through the door that anxious morning, the book they bring provides moral support as it gives us a glimpse into their literary world. Jim brought *Twenty Thousand Leagues Under the Sea* (Verne 1962) and insisted he could read it. Stephanie brought a book her mother had read in second grade. Walter had a book based on the latest Disney movie. Bob brought his most treasured Dr. Seuss.

Favorite books give us the perfect opportunity to introduce reading response sheets. The children bring their books to a circle on the rug. Donna models the sharing procedure as she holds up a favorite picture book, *Our Cat Flossie* (Brown 1986). She invites students to share the title of their book, the author, and why they chose to bring this special book. When every child has had a turn, it is time to introduce the reading response sheet.

This sheet provides a space for an illustration, since second graders may need to draw first to clarify and organize their ideas. It has spaces for writing the title and the author and lines to write two or three sentences about the book.

We talk together and begin a list of what to write on response sheets. Across the top of a large chart paper is written "What We Can Write About Books." We ask the students to think back to what was said about their favorite books. The first item on our list is usually "What we like about a book." This fall the second item was "What the book is about." Our list stalled there until Kristy remembered she had told us about the horse in her book, which was *Black Beauty* (Sewell 1986). We then added "Characters." We thought a bit longer. The children were stumped. What else could you say about a book? Donna smiled to herself. She knew there were many discoveries for her students to make together.

The list of "What We Can Write About Books" stays on the wall for the school year, growing as children realize new possibilities. Morning conversations about picture books provide us with ideas for oral and written responses. By January the list has grown to include:

- special language;
- about the author;
- dislikes;
- favorite part;
- feelings;
- how it is like another book;
- surprises; and
- illustrations.

When Susannah was in fourth grade she came to visit Jane and noticed the chart "What We Can Write about Books" on the closet door. Puzzled, she said, "But that isn't the list we made. I remember when we added 'sense of humor' to it. We thought that was such a great idea because we thought *You Be Good & I'll Be Night* (Merriam 1988) was so funny." Jane was touched that Susannah noticed the new chart and remembered what had occured two years ago.

What Susannah didn't realize was that the list from one year does not serve the next class. Each group of children needs to invent its own. They become mindful of the literary qualities in a book as they create criteria. They begin to understand the significance of what they already

Name Derek

Date 9-24-93

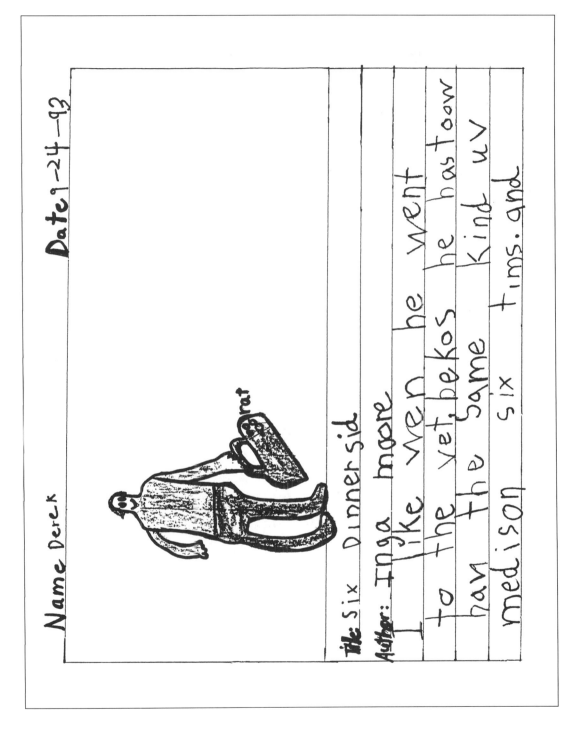

Title: Six Dinner sid

Author: Inga moore

I like wen he went to the vet bekos he has too ov ham the same kind uv medison six tims. and

FIGURE 4–2 Derek's Reading Response Sheet

know. Handing them a list devised by another class can stop thinking and reflection. The process of creating the list is as valuable as the list itself. Inviting all children to participate in this endeavor gives the message that we believe in their ability to discover important ideas. The list in progress confirms the notion that we are a group in progress, growing and becoming better all the time.

After exploring the edges of how to respond to their favorite books, it is time for children to try out their individual ideas. Rachel reads her book as she considers how to write a response. As she chews on the end of her pencil, Jane talks with her about why she likes *Henry and Mudge and the Happy Cat* (Rylant 1990a). Then Jane moves around to help other students and observe them carefully as they work on their first response sheets. When most seem to be finished, the class meets in the circle to share what they have done. Work that is seen only by the teacher does not get the same effort as work that is shared with the class. The response sheet takes on additional currency when children sit in the circle to read what they have written and talk about their illustrations. Positive comments from classmates spur students to improve the quality of their work. This sharing calls attention to the fact that responses to literature are personal and varied.

To help children understand our criteria for response sheets, we ask them to help create a reference chart. This year it said:

What Makes a Good Response Sheet
(writing and illustration)

1. Is your best work
2. Is when you take your time
3. Has colorful pictures
4. Uses details in the writing and the illustrations
5. Uses proper punctuation: periods, question marks
6. Uses capital letters
   to start sentences
   for names

This chart hangs on the closet door. We may refer to it as students begin their reading responses. We encourage our students to be thoughtful workers who set high standards for themselves.

The timing of response writing is flexible. Some children complete a response sheet during a single work period. Others prefer to work on the same response for several days. Because of the varying pace of the students, we may set a minimum requirement for a week, but many children exceed the minimum. For example, when the whole class read *Shoeshine Girl* (Bulla 1988), we asked them to complete five response sheets by the end of the ten chapters. Meredith decided to do a response sheet for each chapter. Walt, a serious young artist, preferred to spend more time on each illustration and completed just the required five response sheets. Since pacing is as personal as losing baby teeth, we build in ways for children to find their own comfort level while doing their best.

As the year progresses, responses become more elaborate and expansive. Details in illustrations show careful thinking about what has been read. Saving samples of response sheets for portfolios makes reading and writing growth visible.

The basic response sheet format may go through revisions as students suggest ways to make it better. Michael, a gifted artist, suggested a larger space for pictures. Rachel requested more lines for writing. Brian wanted a rating scale. We invite our students to initiate changes and improvements in the way we work together. We gladly give credit to those who make suggestions and applaud their initiative. Students come to realize that the teacher is not the only resource for ideas.

As children outgrow their need for a picture space, we offer them a reading journal. New materials are magical for sparking enthusiasm. We use composition books or make journals out of oak tag and lined paper. Decorating the cover of a new journal is a sure way to lead students into the excitement of new books to read.

For days when another rhythm is desirable, a class response sheet can be a successful alternative. Ann Shames, a Westport colleague, writes a question at the top of a sheet of large newsprint; a generic question such as "How did the author pull you into the book?" works best. As her students finish reading their books, they write their name and response to the question. The responses are read and discussed in the group. Students enjoy writing on the oversized paper and reading their words to the class.

Writing questions about literature is not an easy task for second graders. Even though they may have answered and asked many questions orally during book discussions, creating a question can stop many in their tracks. This year when the class read *Shoeshine Girl* (Bulla 1988), Jane gave each student five strips of paper of different colors measuring about two inches by eight and a half inches. Each day as the students read a chapter, they wrote a thoughtful question on one side of the bookmark and their answer on the other with the page number where it was found. The bookmark fit neatly into the book. Energy was high as everyone met in a circle to hear and answer the questions.

Anne Nesbitt helped her second graders learn to recognize good questions. After reading a chapter of *Shoeshine Girl*, they each wrote a question. They met to share their questions and talk about which ones really made them think. The quality of their questions improved dramatically as they met each morning. They moved from literal to inferential questions without knowing about Bloom's Taxonomy.

Children work on book responses daily. To give interest a boost we introduce additional ways to respond. We may use story mapping or small books with a different story element (characters, setting, problem, solution) on each page. Some children like to make story wheels with slices of the wheel telling another event from the story. These are available in the room so readers can decide which kind of response best fits their book and personal inclination. Reader response sheets continue to be used most frequently, but we invite our students to vary their work.

Projects

An administrator visited a new teacher in second grade whose students were busy making projects for their Marc Brown study. "Oh, it must be art time," the administrator commented. To the outside observer, it was difficult to see that reading was taking place. The administrator paused by Mike and Erik to ask about their drawing. They were using the overhead to make a large portrait of Arthur. The boys launched into an explanation of Arthur's personality and how his problems are very much like their own. Yes, the students were thinking in literary ways. Setting aside time for students to pursue artistic interests as they relate to reading gives them the opportunity to think about the connections between reading and their lives.

Projects are an engaging way to signal the close of an author study or a text set unit. We provide the supplies and students provide the ingenuity. Some useful art supplies to have available include construction paper, oak tag, plasticine clay, pipe cleaners, tracing paper, scissors, glue, watercolor and tempera paints, tissue paper, glitter, yarn, fabric scraps, tongue depressors, brown lunch bags, crayons, colored pencils, Craypas, colored chalk, scotch tape, masking tape, needles and thread, hole punches, staplers, staple removers, permanent and washable markers, and old magazines. Parents are excellent sources for some of these materials.

We spend a few minutes before students jump into their projects to list some possibilities Students try to avoid making mistakes because supplies are limited. However, when children set high standards for themselves, we know they may need to start over. Executing a project gives concrete lessons in how to plan and follow through on an idea. Sharing the completed project with the rest of the class provides an opportunity to practice speaking in a more formal setting.

The moments right before cleaning up can be daunting. Will they get the scraps off the floor? Will they get supplies back in their proper places? Second graders can and do take responsibility for cleaning up if they know where things belong and what is expected of them. They surprise us with their efforts at returning the classroom to order, especially when they are looking forward to sharing their own masterpiece.

Author Studies

Our first author study may be suggested by the children on the opening day of school as they bring their favorite books. Or we may choose an author whose books appeal to seven- and eight-year-olds and can be easily read by beginning second graders. Introducing fine pieces of literature is an important goal as we use books to stimulate reading and writing.

We begin by gathering books from the classroom, the public library, and the school library. Students may also have books they wish to lend. As Jane was checking out books from the local public library one day, she met Corey.

COREY: What are you doing with ALL those books, Mrs. Fraser?
JANE: We're going to use them in class.
COREY: I can't wait to see them. Will we start tomorrow?

The entire collection is placed in containers in the reading area. Labels help to keep order among the books, a job that is the responsibility of the children.

Studies of authors illustrate how we provide for choice and flexibility in reading. Students decide

- which books to read.
- whether to work alone or with a partner,
- which group to join,
- what kind of response to write,
- which project to demonstrate what they have learned, and
- how much time to spend with a book.

Author studies are conducted primarily with picture books. Exceptions include the work of Joanna Cole, whose nonfiction writing is sparked with the *Magic School Bus* series (1986–92). Another is Patricia Reilly Giff whose short "chapter books" *The Kids of the Polk Street School* (1984–85) are popular among second graders. Pat Ross's *M & M* series (1985–93), and David Adler's *Cam Jansen* series (1980–93), are authors of longer books children enjoy. Beverly Cleary may be read by some children later in the year after we introduce her books by reading aloud *The Mouse and the Motorcycle* (1965) or *Muggie Maggie* (1990).

An early author study

• creates interest and excitement in reading,
• provides opportunities to talk about book choice,
• offers a variety of books for different reading abilities,
• makes patterns and procedures explicit,
• introduces reading and response strategies,
• begins the brainstormed reference charts,
• creates expertise on authors/illustrators, and
• builds the foundation for independent work.

James Marshall is a favorite author to study early in the year. We share biographical information about James Marshall and give a brief introduction about some of his books. We explain that sometimes Marshall wrote and illustrated the books and at other times he illustrated books written by other authors. *George and Martha* (1972a), *Fox and His Friends* (1982), and *Yummers* (1972b) may be familiar to some of our students, so excitement builds quickly. Josh asked, "Didn't he write *The Stupids Have a Ball*? [Allard 1978]. That is really funny. The Stupids are sooooo stupid!" James Marshall is an easy sell. Suggestions about how we might introduce several James Marshall books follow:

George and Martha (Marshall 1972a). The focus is friendship. Jane might say in class, "Friends try to help each other. Let's look to see how James Marshall shows us that George and Martha are friends." After listening to the story and enjoying the illustrations, children refer back to the text to prove that George and Martha are friends. "Will you turn to the page where George and Martha got out of the basket?" asked Courtney. "They are good friends because even though George was disappointed about not flying, Martha helped him feel better by saying, 'I would rather have you down here with me.' "

Cinderella (Karlin 1989). The focus of the discussion is comparative thinking. Donna might ask, "How does this version of Cinderella compare with others you know? Why do you think James Marshall might have wanted to retell and illustrate this version of the fairy tale?" Corey stated, "That's not how *I* thought Cinderella should look." We ask Corey to use the text and the illustrations to explain her thinking.

The Cut-Ups (Marshall 1984). We begin to push the thinking about the writer's craft by asking "What has the author done to get you interested in this book?" Brian told everyone, "The Cut-Ups act like us. They get in trouble when they didn't do anything wrong."

A clearly visible reading routine is becoming established. We move to the meeting place where children sit comfortably on the rug. A James Marshall book is read aloud each morning. The discussion is focused with a central question or children are asked what they noticed in the text or the illustrations. Following the discussion, students choose any of Marshall's books to read independently. When we introduce a new author we give students time to browse through the collection and chat with each other about the books. We circulate and talk with them as they choose books to read. Once choices are made students find a comfortable place alone or with a partner and settle in to a good book before completing a reading response sheet.

Those who are not comfortable working independently get extra support. We may work with them in a small group. Partner reading is another strategy to assist students who need extra time before they feel ready to read alone. If a stronger and a weaker reader are paired, they can read, discuss a book, and rehearse ideas together as they feed off of each other's thoughts. Jim liked to team up with Alex, a stronger reader. Their working friendship gave him reassurance.

Students keep track of the books they've read with a list of James Marshall titles in their reading folder. The list includes spaces to color in a personal rating on a scale of one to four (see section on rating in Chapter 7).

After James Marshall has been read extensively, we begin the second phase of the author's study. Adults recognize writers, painters, or composers by style. When we see a painting by Monet, we know it is his without looking at the signature. The same is true for authors and illustrators.

We write on chart paper "James Marshall's Fingerprints." Students

BOOKS BY JAMES MARSHALL

Date	Title	Score			
	Fox on Wheels				
	Fox at School				
	Fox Be Nimble				
	Fox in Love				
	Fox All Week				
	Fox on the Job				
	George and Martha				
	George and Martha Encore				
	Rats on the Roof				
	Nosey Mrs. Rat				
	Three Up a Tree				
	Three by the Sea				
	Four on the Shore				
	The Stupids				
	The Stupids Die				
	The Stupids Step Out				
	The Cut-Ups				
	Yummers!				
	Yummers Too				
	Old Mother Hubbard				
	Little Red Riding Hood				
	Cinderella				
		1	2	3	4

FIGURE 4–3 Student Record Keeping for Author Study

Name _____

Find examples to prove each statement about James Marshall.

1.) He is a good writer.
Book_____
Book_____

2.) He uses lots of humor.
Book_____
Book_____

3.) He uses lots of details.
Book_____
Book_____

4.) He writes funny dialogue.
Book_____
Book_____

5.) He really thinks about his writing.

Book_____
Book_____

FIGURE 4–4   Author Study Prove-It

offer their ideas about his characteristics as an author and illustrator. Some of this year's list included:

• He has a sense of humor.
• He likes to use animals as characters.
• He puts surprises in his stories.
• His illustrations can be funny.

Next, the students revisit the books to find proof of their generalizations. To help with organization, we copy their statements onto paper with spaces for writing the titles that support the generalizations.

Megan and Daisy worked together at the round table. They slowly reread each page of *The Stupids Die* (Allard 1981) and studied the illustrations as they looked for evidence to prove the statements. They loved returning to the book as detectives.

Students come to consider themselves experts on authors. One day Nathan said, "I was in the library. I glanced at a book. Before I picked it up, I knew it was a James Marshall book. It was the way the picture looked and the colors he used."

The class compiles a collection of response sheets about an author for the classroom library. The children each choose one they are proud to contribute. Two student editors work with the teacher to edit the individual response sheets contributed by classmates. The completed sheets are spiral bound. When children edit the work of others they often become better editors of their own writing.

The third and final stage of the author study allows students to share what they have learned by doing a project. They may make book posters, bookmarks, write and perform a play, work on a readers' theater script, or create a diorama. Hallie was excited—"I love my Fox puppet. He makes the character seem real." When a student or a group of students completes a project, it is presented to the class. Doing a small performance or talking about project work taps into different skills such as

• honing performance skills,
• summarizing thinking and work,
• creating new forms,
• stirring up interest, and
• cooperating with a group.

Performances may call for a celebration with popcorn or simple refreshments.

Discussion is a core component for author studies and text sets. Discussion times vary greatly. They may be brief, with only one or two children sharing. They may be longer, with time given for everyone in the circle to share. We have sign-up sheets kept in a central place and keep track of the activities in our journals to be sure no one is being overlooked. Jane's journal indicated that Samantha had been quiet over a period of weeks. Jane privately asked her to think about contributing at the next share, giving the message that her ideas were valued.

When patterns for author studies are well established, we may have books by several authors in the classroom to allow for individual flexibility. Projects on a number of authors keep interest high and provide for varying abilities and paces in reading and responding to literature. Brian, who worked quickly and thoroughly, studied and enjoyed Jane Yolen, especially the *Commander Toad* series (1980–87). When he was finished he was considering the books of James Stevenson and turned to Jesse, who was reading Stevenson. Brian said, "I might like to read those books. I notice James Stevenson uses cartoons. Are they funny?"

Children begin to broaden our ideas of choice. Tim went to the public library, checked out a group of books by Chris van Allsburg, and brought them to the classroom for study. Jordan decided to read all the *Horrible Harry* (1988–92) books by Suzy Kline.

When students are involved in other reading work (such as learning adventures or book groups), we may read aloud books that the students are not reading on their own. For example, Kevin Henkes is a favorite author/illustrator, but his titles are not extensive enough for an author study in the usual format. Instead, we read aloud one of his books each morning; discuss the qualities of his writing, illustrations, and story events; and discuss how his book relates to our lives. *Julius, the Baby of the World* (1989), *Chester's Way* (1988), and *Chrysanthemum* (1991) delight the children and guarantee dynamic discussions. Each day we add to our growing knowledge of Henkes's work. After we have read all his books aloud, we review what we know and vote on our favorite book. The books are kept on the chalkrail for students to read if they wish. They move from child to child and rarely get a rest.

Bill Peet and William Steig are two other favorite author/illustrators who lend themselves to being read aloud by the teacher since the vocabulary is challenging for many students and the length of the stories might be intimidating. Hearing the stories read, however, turns most students into Peet and Steig fans.

Text Sets

A text set is a thematic collection of books. The books may be fiction or nonfiction and picture or chapter books. The size of a text set is limited only by available titles and our imagination. Work with text sets follows a pattern similar to author studies. We collect books, introduce them to our students, encourage browsing, structure questions, read aloud, share, and allow for student choices. Students read, share, complete response sheets, and share again. Reading time is divided into chunks to provide for these activities.

Typical Reading Period for an Author Study or Text Set

8:55– 9:05 AM:	Read aloud from picture book
9:05– 9:15 AM:	Discussion of book
9:15–10:00 AM:	Individual reading and response writing
	• Children read silently or in small groups.
	• Children write response sheet or journal entry.
	• Teacher meets with individuals or small groups.
	• Children work on personal reading or writing when response is completed.
10:00–10:15 AM:	Circle time to share responses

This chart indicates how chunks of time are divided. In practice the schedule is flexible.

As we plan a text set we consider its integration with our curriculum. We use every opportunity that will point toward a genuine combination of disciplines and make the classroom a closer replica of life. If children are studying environmental issues in science, a text set weaves together reading and science. Text sets about animals serve the interests of our science curriculum and students. Jesse, who was myopic, had been told by his family that he was blind as a bat. When he read *Animal Fact, Animal Fable* (Simon 1979), he was ecstatic. "I can't wait to tell my sister, bats aren't blind. I just learned that bats can see insects at night."

A text set dealing with language fascinates this age group. Books about Amelia Bedelia (Parish 1964–93) appeal to a seven- and eight-year-old sense of humor and lend themselves to language talk. Verna Aardema uses unusual words to describe sounds in her African tales.

Her books provoke interesting ideas that carry over into student writing. Jane Yolen's *Commander Toad* books lead to discussions about puns. *Chicka Chicka Boom Boom* (Martin and Archambault 1987) is an example of another kind of playfulness with language.

In September and early October we may study alphabet books. Collecting them is easy and fun. A wide variety provides for a range of student interest and ability. Examples of this variety include *Eating the Alphabet* (Ehlert 1989), *Alligators All Around* (Sendak 1962), *The Z was Zapped* (van Allsburg 1987), *Anno's Alphabet* (Anno 1975), and *Jambo Means Hello* (Feelings 1974).

At the conclusion of this experience the class makes an "alphabet big book" using an art technique we learned from Sue Bambach, a primary teacher in Westport. Students outline their picture lightly in pencil first. Next they use a black fine-line permanent marker over the pencil lines. The final step is to color the drawings with watercolors. This makes a beautiful illustration. The big book has a page for each letter of the alphabet. We write the letters, upper- and lowercase, on the blank pages. Children choose which letter they wish to illustrate, often the one at the beginning of their first name. We brainstorm ideas in the large group to give help. Sharing our completed alphabet book is the final step. Younger children in kindergarten and first grade are a natural audience. This big book becomes part of our classroom library to be read and enjoyed throughout the school year.

Fairy and folk tales make excellent text sets. *Bony Legs* (Cole 1983), *The Crystal Apple* (McDermott 1974), *The Three Sillies* (Galdone 1981), and *Goldilocks and the Three Bears* (Marshall 1988) are part of a text set that reaches all reading levels. Andrew and Sean are both interested in *St. George and the Dragon* (Hodges 1984). Sean does not want to read it independently so they read and discuss it together. They work on their response sheets and help each other with ideas.

Text sets may combine fiction and nonfiction. Anne Nesbitt, our second-grade colleague, organized a set of fiction books about bears that included *Corduroy* (Freeman 1968), *Jesse Bear, What Will You Wear?* (Carlstrom 1986), and *Little Bear* (Minarik 1957). She also created a nonfiction book set that included *Bears* (Barrett 1990) and *White Bear, Ice Bear* (Ryder 1989). As children read and talked about the books, they made a list of ways the two sets were different. They discussed how we read fiction and nonfiction and when we might decide to read one or the other. Anne's students discovered they could tell if a book was fiction or nonfiction from the title and cover illustration.

Several text sets in the room will allow for a variety of interest and abilities. We spend time giving book talks and encouraging students to browse and talk with each other before they choose which set to study. Groups are formed. They are probably different in membership from any previous groups for reading. Because children like organization, they are eager to appoint a leader and a recorder. Each group talks about how they wish to proceed. At the end of the work period, each group told their plans:

Nathan's group: We decided to read the books together.
Sophie's group: We're going to read with a partner and discuss the
    books together.
Alex's group: We're going to read the books on our own and each
    write a question.

Spirited discussions help to hold interest in a text set. We circulate during reading time and make sure that everyone is feeling good about personal participation in the group. We coach students to ask questions that promote thinking, good discussion, and evaluation.

Gathering together as a class and sharing what is happening in the separate groups is important. Interest is generated when class members hear about the books others are reading. When the groups next reported, they said,

Nathan's group: We read part of *The Unhuggables* [National Wildlife
    Federation 1988]. We liked the disgusting pictures, especially the
    wasps and the bats.
Sophie's group: Ashley and I think people should pick up their garbage
    [they were reading *A Tale of Antarctica* (Glimmerveen 1989)].
    Jessica and Kat read *Rain Forest Secrets* [Dorros 1990]. It was too
    long. They think it has lots of information but they couldn't get
    so interested in it.
Alex's group: Writing questions is hard. We decided to each tell one
    thing we learned. Paul thought it was surprising that a supermarket
    uses seven hundred paper bags in less than an hour [they were
    reading *50 Simple Things Kids Can Do to Save The Earth* (The
    Earthworks Group 1990)].

Using text sets offers a broad variety of books for students. Text sets are a good organizing technique for integrating the curriculum while teaching reading skills and strategies.

Nonfiction

The picture book we read aloud to begin the day may relate to themes in science and social studies. School programs or field trips call for additional information. When our classes took a fall walk through a nearby forest, *How the Forest Grew* (Jaspersohn 1980) gave the students an awareness that the forest had changed over time.

Reading nonfiction can enable students to pursue an individual interest or passion, allowing them to focus on their own personal strengths as learners. Donna introduces learning adventures, a research project that takes at least three weeks to complete. The children make individual lists of things they would like to learn. Later in the week they revisit their lists and narrow them to one topic. Ashley knew immediately that her choice would be horses. Alex wanted to learn about snakes. There is a lot of work ahead, so topics must be cared about.

Once topics have been selected, Donna hands out oak tag and white paper journals. On the first page students list three facts they already know about their topic followed by three "I wonder" questions. The children will write in the journal each day as they track their thinking and progress. A reference chart hangs in a prominent place:

Learning Adventure Steps

1. Research your topic and jot down notes.
2. Write five interesting facts to share.
3. Have Mrs. S. check for spelling and capitals.
4. Put lined paper under overhead sheet and copy facts in your best printing.
5. Complete your art project.
6. Share with pride.

Lucy McCormick Calkins coined the phrase "learning adventure." It captures the spirit of fun in the learning process. Because second graders have so many interests, turning them loose with a learning adventure is an exciting way to let them pursue their curiosity while they grow as readers and writers.

The first job is to fill the room with books that children can read. Donna visits the public library to check out books. She encourages students to do the same in the school library. Arielle and Alex arrive the next morning loaded down with *Zoo Books* and *Ranger Rick*. The spectacular photographs invite young researchers to get going. After a quick lesson in using an index, they are off. Reading time speeds by as students locate magazines and books about their topic. Clipboards come out of desks and children sprawl around the room absorbed in their reading and note-taking. The enthusiasm is contagious.

Once they have read and written down as much information as they can, the researchers reread their facts and select the five they think are the most interesting and surprising, a selection process that forces them to reconsider what they have jotted down from books and magazines. The facts are written on an overhead transparency or chart paper to be used for presentation to the group. Sharing the facts in written form pushes students to a higher standard of content and written conventions.

Next, students begin an art project to represent what they have learned. Overhead transparencies are a new, exciting material. By placing the transparency over a photograph, students can trace it, color it in, and have an accurate rendering of their topic. Placed on the overhead projector, the illustrations look impressive. Some children prefer another kind of project and are encouraged to make a different choice. Perhaps they will work with clay, make mobiles, or create posters about their topic.

We invite another second-grade class to our learning adventure presentations. Students tell about their topic and why they chose it. With the transparency in place, the five facts are read, followed by showing the transparency drawing. "Oooohs" and "aahhs" can be heard.

Chase and Arielle worked together on rabbits since both have a pet rabbit at home. They completed a mobile, an overhead transparency, and clay replicas of their own bunnies. They gave their presentation dressed in white, wearing bunny ears and tails they made. Not all presentations are that elaborate, but everyone takes them seriously.

Learning adventures allow students to go as far as they are able. Some students need more support while others take off without a backward glance. Arthur was one of this year's surprises. He was a bright student whose performance did not often match his potential. A space and aircraft buff, he was the last to share his learning adventure. He had not been able to write five facts but he had an overhead transparency with drawings of UFOs, his chosen topic. His drawings contained intricate details. As he spoke to the audience, his voice took on authority and confidence. He looked around the room as he spoke and talked in a comfortable, natural way as if he were a regular keynote speaker at conferences. "You're not going to believe this," he said, "but I think I may have seen a UFO."

The children laughed. He laughed with them. "I told you you wouldn't believe it. But let me tell you about it." He had their complete attention as he proceeded to tell his story and the facts about several other sightings. He took Donna's breath away. This was a side of Arthur she had not seen until today, the last week of school. Where had this ability and confidence come from? Donna rejoiced that she had such an opportunity, an opportunity that nearly slipped away as the year drew to a close.

Donna's class did learning adventures in January and in June. The final learning adventure project kept the students engaged and active the last two weeks of the school year. Students were involved, enthusiastic, and still willing to learn as summer days approached. The last entry in their journals agreed with Donna's informal evaluation: The students felt proud of their efforts and enjoyed the independence of working on their own topics.

Long-range activities that allow students to make choices, pace themselves, and work independently honor their budding maturity. We are there with a safety net if anyone reaches too far, but usually they extend themselves beyond former boundaries and still attain success. Jane reflected on learning adventures in her journal:

> I didn't realize that seven year olds could become so involved in research. When I was doing staff development I noticed that second-grade boys loved to read and discuss nonfiction. Now I see that doing research on a self-chosen topic is a meaningful learning experience. In fourth grade, years ago, we asked the children to do research reports. They worked more than two months in lockstep fashion without choice or spontaneity. The emphasis was on the final product, not the learning. It was a negative experience for the less capable students, who found the process defeating. The way we are doing it now makes nonfiction reading more personal and informative. The kids are excited and love the change of pace. When they do their presentations I realize again that we truly understand something when we teach it to others.

Whole Class Novels
Reading a novel together is a change of pace. The class reads, discusses, and responds to a novel that we have in multiple paperback copies. *Shoeshine Girl* (Bulla 1988) and *Stay Away from Simon* (Carrick 1985)

are two novels we have successfully used. They were chosen for the discussions they stimulate about relationships, behavior, values, and attitudes. Both books have short chapters and are about eighty pages in length. *Stay Away from Simon* offers information about life in early New England, which integrates nicely with our social studies curriculum.

The class reads a novel in the late winter or early spring when most children are ready for an easy chapter book. It provides a further check on reading skills, strategies, and comprehension. Children who are unable to read on their own are paired or we work with them in a group. In this voluntary group we read sections aloud as they follow the text. Everyone is included in this experience of reading a novel.

Students read each chapter independently and write a response in their journal. Then the chapter is discussed and analyzed by the class. If Lindsay has read ahead she is asked not to make predictions or tell any surprises. Children can be trusted to honor these requests. Discussions are lively as children develop respect for the point of view of others.

Using a novel with the whole class is an excellent time to teach skills in context. As we focus on a particular passage, we ask everyone to turn to that page. A volunteer reads a chunk of text. After this reading, we may discuss vocabulary, a figure of speech, an expression, foreshadowing, or character development. This discussion gives our students new strategies for responding to their reading. Second-grade discussions echo the same talks we have in our adult book groups. It is thrilling to see how our students latch onto an idea like foreshadowing as they integrate it into their understanding of the author's craft. After a discussion about foreshadowing in *Stay Away from Simon,* Jacqueline blurted out "Oh, I just found some foreshadowing. Maggie is reading the teacher's notes in cursive. She's getting interested in it" (from *Muggie Maggie* [Cleary 1990]).

During the discussions of the novel we use a modification of the strategy mentioned in the section about author studies. Allison stated, "Sarah Ida [*Shoeshine Girl*] is really unhappy being with her Aunt Claudia." We ask her to read a passage from the text to prove her point. This is a check on reading comprehension and fluency. Before Allison reads she tells everyone what page and what paragraph she plans to read aloud. Everyone in the class reads silently as Allison reads aloud. Locating text has given us the opportunity to teach students how to recognize a paragraph and to discuss why and how paragraphs are organized.

Many seven- and eight-year-olds need guidance to understand dialogue and how quotation marks work. Children read some pages of the novel like readers' theater. We duplicate a page or two for everyone and ask students to highlight parts for each reader. The connecting text such as "Jim said" and "asked John" is eliminated with a marker. This makes the dialogue clear and the reading easier. Soon students can read without the text highlighted and connecting words marked out. Pairs of students take turns performing the text. Arielle and Kristen practiced their parts so well that the characters came alive for the rest of the class.

Children may keep a special notebook for their written responses about a novel. Discussion precedes writing. We raise the level of comprehension and written response by pooling ideas. These special journals provide an ongoing record of a student's responses to the novel. Sara told everyone "I like to read what I wrote yesterday before I write in my journal. It helps me get started." Her strategy was adopted by others.

Reading a whole class novel introduces a new atmosphere, adding variety to the patterns we have established earlier in the year. We pace our study of each chapter carefully with the aim of moving along at a rate appropriate to eight-year-olds who prefer activities that move quickly. At the same time we satisfy the demand for rigor in the discussion of the novel and the author's craft. Children who had not done so before begin to think of novels as a choice for personal reading.

What are we doing during reading time? We may be

- sitting with a response group as they discuss a book or an author,
- helping a group decide what they wish to present to the class,
- listening to a student read as we diagnose how to help improve personal reading skills,
- assisting children with book selection,
- helping students make decisions about their reader response,
- working on a skill in the context of a story (such as a phonics element) with a group of children,
- asking someone comprehension questions designed to assess the ability to infer or make predictions,
- nudging a child to expand a reading response or think of it in a new way, and
- doing echo reading with a student in a way designed to improve fluency.

Our goal in the teaching of reading is to promote independent and confident readers who know what they like to read. We introduce a wide variety of literature to extend reading repertoires. We share ideas about reading that are adapted and integrated by our students.

Whatever activity we plan, there are choices to be made by seven- and eight-year-old readers. There is movement in the room. There are conversations and sharing. There are questions to be raised. There is reading and writing to do.

From the beginning of the year we have established consistent patterns. This is a comfort for children this age. They need to know what to expect. Children know that reading is a workshop time and they are always working to become better readers. If children are finished with their reading and their written response before it is time to share, they have many choices available. They have learned that they may

- read,
- write,
- work in poetry journals (see Chapter 5),
- write a letter to a friend or relative,
- go to the school library,
- plan subsequent reading activities, or
- work at the computer.

Reading is the time when we use all our strategic practices. We are constantly aware of metacognitive thinking as we develop our students' abilities to respond to literature. We encourage choice and flexibility. We look for ways to integrate learning. We demonstrate trust and focus on the strengths of our learners as we allow our seven- and eight-year-olds to pursue their individual goals. We strive to connect our teaching to the lives of our students while listening to reader responses and evaluations. We model, encourage language conversations, and try to make our criteria explicit. We encourage cooperation, collaboration, and shared decision-making.

The kindergarten and first-grade experiences of our young readers have helped prepare them for the next stages in their development. We are gratified to watch the quiet first graders who enter our classes in September emerge in June as independent and confident children. They have eagerly accepted our gift—the love for literature.

References

Aardema, Verna. 1975. *Why Mosquitoes Buzz in People's Ears*. New York: Scholastic.

Adler, David A. 1980–93. *Cam Jansen* series. New York: Viking.

Allard, Harry. 1978. *The Stupids Have a Ball*. Boston: Houghton Mifflin.

———. 1981. *The Stupids Die*. Boston: Houghton Mifflin.

Anno, Mitsumasa. 1975. *Anno's Alphabet: An Adventure in Imagination*. New York: HarperCollins.

Barrett, Norman. 1990. *Bears*. New York: Watts, Franklin.

Brown, Ruth. 1986. *Our Cat Flossie*. New York: Dutton.

Bulla, Clyde. 1988. *Shoeshine Girl*. New York: The Trumpet Club.

Carlstrom, Nancy White. 1986. *Jesse Bear, What Will You Wear?* New York: Macmillan.

Carrick, Carol. 1985. *Stay Away from Simon*. New York: Clarion Books.

Cleary, Beverly. New York: 1965. *The Mouse and the Motorcycle*. New York: Morrow Junior Books.

———. 1990. *Muggie Maggie*. New York: Morrow Junior Books.

Cole, Joanna. 1983. *Bony-Legs*. New York: Four Winds Press.

———. 1986–92. *Magic School Bus* series. New York: Scholastic.

Dorros, Arthur. 1990. *Rain Forest Secrets*. New York: Scholastic.

Earth Works Group. 1990. *50 Simple Things Kids Can Do to Save the Earth*. Kansas City, MO: Andrews and McMeel.

Ehlert, Lois. 1989. *Eating the Alphabet: Fruits and Vegetables from A to Z*. San Diego Harcourt Brace Jovanovich.

Feelings, Muriel. 1974. *Jambo Means Hello: Swahili Alphabet Book*. New York: Harper & Row.

Freeman, Don. 1968. *Corduroy*. New York: Viking.

Galdone, Paul. 1981. *The Three Sillies*. New York: Clarion Books.

Gannett, Ruth S. 1987. *My Father's Dragon*. New York: Knopf.

Giff, Patricia Reilly. 1984–85. *The Kids of the Polk Street School* series. New York: Dell.

Glimmerveen, Ulco. 1989. *A Tale of Antarctica*. New York: Scholastic.

Henkes, Kevin. 1988. *Chester's Way*. New York: Greenwillow Books.

———. 1989. *Julius, the Baby of the World*. New York: Greenwillow Books.

———. 1991. *Chrysanthemum*. New York: Greenwillow Books.

Hodges, Margaret. 1984. *Saint George and the Dragon: A Golden Legend*. Boston: Little, Brown.

Jaspersohn, William. 1980. *How the Forest Grew*. New York: Greenwillow Books.

Karlin, Barbara. 1989. *Cinderella*. Boston: Little, Brown.

Kline, Suzy. 1988–92. *Horrible Harry* series. New York: Viking Kestrel.

————. 1992. *Herbie Jones and the Dark Attic*. New York: G. P. Putnam's.

McDermott, Beverly. 1974. *The Crystal Apple*. New York: Viking.

Marshall, Edward. 1982. *Fox and His Friends*. New York: Dial Press.

Marshall, James. 1972a. *George and Martha*. Boston: Houghton Mifflin.

————. 1972b. *Yummers*. Boston: Houghton Mifflin.

————. 1984. *The Cut-Ups*. New York: Viking Kestrel.

————. 1988. *Goldilocks and the Three Bears*. New York: Dial Books for Young Readers.

Martin, Bill, Jr., and John Archambault. 1987. *Chicka Chicka Boom Boom*. New York: Henry Holt.

Merriam, Eve. 1988. *You Be Good & I'll Be Night*. New York: Morrow Junior Books

Minarik, Else Homelund. 1957. *Little Bear*. New York: Harper & Row.

National Wildlife Federation. 1988. *The Unhuggables*. Washington, D.C.

Parish, Peggy. 1964–93. *Amelia Bedelia* series. New York: Harper & Row and New York: Greenwillow.

Parsons, Alexandra. 1990. *Amazing Snakes*. Eyewitness Jr. Books. New York: Random House.

Peet, Bill. 1984. *Cowardly Clyde*. Boston: Houghton Mifflin.

Ross, Pat. 1985–93. *M & M* series. New York: Puffin.

Ryder, Joanne. 1989. *White Bear, Ice Bear*. New York: Morrow Jr. Books.

Rylant, Cynthia. 1990a. *Henry and Mudge and the Happy Cat*. New York: Bradbury Press.

————. 1990b. *Henry and Mudge in Puddle Trouble*. New York: Bradbury Press.

Sendak, Maurice. 1962. *Alligators All Around: An Alphabet*. New York: Harper & Row.

Sewell, Anna. 1986. *Black Beauty*. New York: Random House.

Simon, Seymour. 1979. *Animal Fact, Animal Fable*. New York: Crown.

Smith, Janice Lee. 1988. *The Show-and-Tell War and Other Stories about Adam Joshua*. New York: Harper & Row.

Steig, William. 1988. *Spinky Sulks*. New York: Farrar, Straus and Giroux.

Thaler, Mike. 1989. *Teacher from the Black Lagoon*. New York: Scholastic.

van Allsburg, Chris. 1987. *The Z Was Zapped*. Boston: Houghton Mifflin.

Verne, Jules. 1962. *Twenty Thousand Leagues Under the Sea*. New York: Macmillan.

White, E. B. 1952. *Charlotte's Web*. New York: Harper & Row.

Yolen, Jane. 1980–87. *Commander Toad* series. New York: Coward, McCann and Geoghegan.

Pass That Book Again 5

  The pattern of our reading classrooms is dependable but not so repetitive as to be drudgery. We understand the need for new books, materials that vary, responses that can be creative, and chunks of time that allow for either interaction or quiet.

Students brought their favorite books with them to school the opening day. Jim, for instance, carried *Twenty Thousand Leagues Under the Sea* and told everyone he could read it. Jim had signaled to Jane that he needed help with book selection.

Choosing a book is a skill that second graders need to develop. Why waste time with a book that is unappealing or too difficult to savor? There are so many books available for young and emergent readers, it is not hard to steer each child down the path toward reading pleasure.

When children learn to make good choices they are on their way. We help by reading aloud as much as possible. We share a wide variety of our treasured children's books and discuss these books to enhance understanding and pleasure. We talk about the ways we select books and make certain there is a wide and changing selection of books available in the classroom.

But first and foremost, we provide opportunities for our students to read. That is the priority work to be done during reading class and the best way we know to help children become better readers. One of those opportunities is our daily independent reading time.

Independent Reading
From the beginning of the school year we expect every student to read independently every day. This is a keystone of our reading program.

We schedule a daily time when children select and read a book of their choice. Some plan ahead for this reading period while others are more impulsive as they scoop up books to read at the last minute. The impulsivity lessens as the year progresses and our students plan more thoughtfully for personal reading.

Daily silent reading provides opportunities for children to improve their reading skills. We discuss the importance of practice with a sports analogy. Second graders understand that you become a better bike rider by riding a bike. You improve your soccer skills by playing the game. From the first day of school when we request that each student bring a favorite book from home, we encourage our students to keep a book handy in their desks. Our purpose is to help children develop the habits of lifelong readers. Jane's journal contains the following entry about independent reading:

> I used to think that independent reading required total silence and that I needed to model my love of reading at that time. Now I feel that this is a great opportunity to diagnose and teach or get ready to teach. I can observe book choice to see if it is appropriate. I can see patterns of book choice and make suggestions for broadening a child's reading range. I can talk with a student to better understand his thinking about, for example, the characters, the illustrations, or the problem and its solution. As I move around the quiet room, the individual attention I can give to a child is a luxury not easily found in a hectic school day.
>
> Today I discovered that Jana's miscues are inappropriate and that Tom skips so many words that the omissions interfere with his comprehension. I need to help them develop better strategies for reading words they don't know. Jana and Tom could form a small group with Sami and Jake, who are afraid to choose a book which looks difficult. They would all benefit from time thinking about the questions: What can I do when I come to a word or group of words I don't know, and, Is it important to know every word in a text I am reading?

In the beginning of the year silent reading lasts five minutes. By the end of the year when reading ends after thirty to forty minutes, loud groans can be heard. Parents tell us that silent reading interest and time increase at home as well. The better young readers become, the more they enjoy practicing their skills. The circle begins to spiral—up, up, and away.

"Popcorn reading" became a favorite ritual in Donna's class. The last Friday of the month was set aside for thirty minutes of silent reading accompanied by a bowl of popcorn. The atmosphere in the room was similar to an evening in front of the fireplace. Chase wrote a letter to Donna at the end of the year that said, "My favorite thing in class was sitting down with a good book and reading for half an hour with popcorn." It was a relaxing, special time together.

Interest for independent reading is stimulated in reading and writing shares when we read aloud and give book talks. After we read an especially interesting book such as *The Magic School Bus Lost in the Solar System* (Cole 1990), many wish to read it themselves. One day when competition for a book was high, Ashley suggested to everyone that we use a sign-up sheet. She neatly solved a problem that had bothered us all year.

Shared reading at home is another independent reading strategy. This shared reading is voluntary. We send a letter home to find out who wishes to participate in this activity. The plan is for a student and parent to read together a book chosen by the child. After reading, both child and parent write a response in a journal. To facilitate this activity, we staple together an oak-tag cover with about eight pages of notebook paper. Students decorate the covers. The journals go home on Monday and are returned to school on Friday with the new entries. It is interesting to read journal responses from the parent and the child. We add a brief comment or suggest another related book the student might enjoy.

What children read independently is integrated into the reading classroom. We listen carefully as Mike talks about his current book, *Tut's Mummy Lost—and Found* (Donnelly 1988). We check in with Brian to find out why he is so interested in the biography of Louis Braille (Davidson 1991). We encourage both of them to share their thoughts in the larger group when we have an independent reading share.

MIKE: They couldn't find Tut's tomb. They lost it for a long time. Then they found it and the mummy was still there with lots of gold things, too.

BRIAN: Louis Braille was this blind guy who invented a way for blind people to read. It is an alphabet that sticks up on paper so you can feel it with your fingers. See, this is what it looks like (showing the class).

Seven- and eight-year-olds are serious and fluent as they talk about books and give their classmates ideas about what to read. Students ask telling questions as they try to decide if they are interested in a particular book.

Reading Aloud

We read aloud to start both the morning and the afternoon. This reading begins the first morning of the school year. Reading aloud is a favorite time for our students and for us. We read with dramatic flair and imagine our performances to be Oscar material. Donna's favorite voice is the Wicked Witch of the West. Jane likes to be the sheep in *Babe the Gallant Pig* (King-Smith 1985).

Reading aloud embodies our beliefs in sharing the world of stories with children, immersing students in language, and building a community through shared literary experiences. A day without reading aloud is like a day without smiles.

Each morning we read a picture book, showing the illustrations as we move through the pages. Our choices vary widely. The book may be written by an author being studied by the class. When the Caldecott winner is announced or a colleague shows us a new book or an event in the room demands a specific title, we begin our morning with that book. Frank wrote about splitting his week between his mother's apartment and his father's house. *Charlie Anderson* (Abercrombie 1990) had to be the next book we read. Stacy worried about some mean fourth graders on the bus. *Loudmouth George and the Sixth Grade Bully* (Carlson 1983) introduced a necessary discussion about bullies.

When students arrive back from lunch and recess with smudged faces and loud voices, reading aloud quickly transforms the room into a safe, comfortable nest. For this read-aloud time we choose a chapter book. The first book of the year may be *My Father's Dragon* (Gannett 1987b), a classic that grabs students on the first page and doesn't let them go until the third book in the series is finished later in the month. This story time is not followed by written responses or assignments. This is a time, like those moments before going to bed, when students can relax into the story, assured that no demands will be made of them beyond quiet listening.

Before we begin to read our chapter book, we mention what was happening when we stopped. We ask a student to recap the story for those who were absent. We may read the chapter title and ask for predictions about what might happen, discussing and making explicit with our students what we do ourselves as a reader. Reading chapter books aloud encourages second graders to read longer books. Many choose to reread a book on their own after they have heard it read aloud. As Jane's journal notes,

> Read-aloud time is a time of magic. The children sit dazzled
> by the story, whether it is a Beverly Cleary novel, a Roald

Dahl caper, or a classic like *Winnie the Pooh*. I feel a great responsibility to introduce my students to classics. They are familiar with Pooh or *The Wonderful Wizard of Oz*, but they know only the movie versions. They are amazed to learn about the original versions. I especially love to flaunt my second edition copy of *The Wizard* with its old-fashioned illustrations.

When we vote for book of the week [see Chapter 9] they always seem to prefer a chapter book if there is one among the choices. These longer, more sustained stories are class favorites.

Reading longer books influences book choice. More children reach for the stars after they become intrigued by the magic of a master storyteller and a more complex plot.

Our favorite, tried-and-true read-aloud books are listed below.

- Frank L. Baum. *The Wonderful Wizard of Oz*.
- Judy Blume. *Tales of a Fourth Grade Nothing*.
- ————. *Superfudge*.
- Beverly Cleary. *The Mouse and the Motorcycle*.
- ————. *Muggie Maggie*.
- ————. *Runaway Ralph*.
- Roald Dahl. *Fantastic Mr. Fox*.
- Russell Erickson. *A Toad for Tuesday*.
- Ruth Gannett. *The Dragon of Blueland*.
- ————. *Elmer and the Dragon*.
- ————. *My Father's Dragon*.
- Dick King-Smith. *Babe the Gallant Pig*.
- Katherine Leverich. *Best Enemies*.
- ————. *Best Enemies, Again*.
- Lois Lowry. *All About Sam*.
- Robert McCloskey. *Homer Price*.
- A. A. Milne. *Winnie the Pooh*.
- Louis Sachar. *The Sideways Stories of Wayside School*.
- Janice Smith. *The Show-and-Tell War: And Other Stories about Adam Joshua*.
- Laura Ingalls Wilder. *Little House in the Big Woods*.

The Reference Chart

Another idea we introduce that busy first day is the reference chart. We ask children to jot down two rules they would like for our class.

Jane moves to the chart stand and writes the words "Our Class Rules" across the top of the paper. Students contribute their ideas.

JAMIE: We should try to be nice to everyone.
TIM: It is good to take care of our things.
JESSE: Everyone should help with cleanup when we are finished with a job.
ADAM: I think we should try to do our best work.

Reference charts are brainstormed by the class. They make our criteria for reading, responding, writing, and behavior explicit. Their power is that they are developed by group consensus. While there is a remarkable similarity from year to year, the children in the classroom have "invented" the criteria themselves. They own them. In November, Ashley and Kristen asked to decorate a chart. After this, many young artists were involved in making our reference charts more attractive and colorful.

A chart on "Being a Good Listener" spells out the expectations for listening behavior. A chart of special language verifies that we are looking for variety in writing. As we study idioms, we keep an ongoing list. Children add idioms they discover in their reading, in conversations, and on TV. One day Courtney said, "I heard an idiom last night. My dad told me 'Money doesn't grow on trees.' And I knew what he meant."

As our students use the charts for reference, they are being initiated into the concept of using reference materials. For example, Katherine had difficulty spelling the word *character*, which she liked to use in her written responses. When Jane pointed out that the word was on a wall chart, Katherine was proud to spell the word correctly. Or again, when the class was discussing James Marshall's characteristics as an author/illustrator, Jamie said, "James Marshall puts details in his pictures which he doesn't write in the story. The pictures give us more information." David responded excitedly, "That's another thing we can write about, the details in the illustrations and what we learn from them." The purple marker came out and a new idea was added to the chart "What Can We Write About Books?"

Reference charts are an integral part of teaching reading and writing. These charts decorate our rooms, becoming more numerous as the year progresses. Some are finished pieces, like poems, that we have copied onto chart paper, but many are works in progress. Students quickly learn that our charts are there to be revised and expanded. We will discuss these charts again in Chapters 6, 7, 8, and

9. The following list gives a sample of the charts that we may create in our classrooms:

- Class Rules
- What Makes a Good Story?
- How I Have Changed as a Reader
- Rules for Sharing
- How to Write About Illustrations
- Characters in Stories
- A Good Response Sheet. . . .
- What Can We Write About Books?
- Elements of Fairy Tales and Folk Tales
- An Author's or Illustrator's Fingerprints
- Questions for Chapter Books
- Writing Tips
- Story Ideas Come from. . . .
- What Writers Do
- Being a Good Listener
- Idioms
- What Do I Do When I Am Finished?
- What Is a Good Question?

Poetry

Poetry brings energy into our classrooms. It is an example of the strategic practice we call "connected teaching." We choose poems that relate to our lives. When we study snails and watch them crawl on desks and over pencils, students learn "Snail" (Drinkwater 1989). Dark and dreary December is made more tolerable by the beautiful line from "I Heard a Bird Sing in the Dark of December": "We are nearer to spring than we were in September" (Herford 1988). A shelf of poetry books stands ready to offer lyrical or humorous words for all occasions.

Several years ago we had the privilege of attending a two-day poetry workshop with Myra Cohn Livingston, Karla Kuskin, X. J. Kennedy, Charlotte Zolotow, and Lee Bennett Hopkins. Their messages rang loud and clear. Children should be given the freedom to follow their own wishes and not be required to write poetry. Poetry should be a part of daily life in the classroom and not be taught for only one week each year. These poets helped us understand that our job is to help children see that poetry is all around us and to help them make unexpected connections.

The influence of Don Graves, Bill Martin, Jr., and David Booth can be seen in the many poems that we print on chart paper that are decorated with student artwork. The first day of school we recite "Boa Constrictor" (Silverstein 1974a). Those who are familiar with it proudly join in. Rarely a day passes that does not include a poem or two. Our distant mentors taught us that children will easily remember poems if they are repeated once or twice over a series of days. Memorizing becomes natural and unnoticed and results in a sense of pride. As Jane notes in her journal,

> It is fun to begin the day with a rousing poem. It is clarion wake-up call as it brings us together—a shared delight. After practicing a poem several times, everyone can read it. Reading poetry, with its predictability, supports every reader. The quick shot of meter at the beginning of the day, or before lunch, or at dismissal time is a great community building activity.

Jane's husband grew up in Hungary. A friend asked him recently if he still speaks Hungarian. "No," he said, "but I can recite poetry and sing songs." Poems seep into our long-term memory and stay with us.

Students collect their own favorite poems in a personal poetry journal that stays in a bin on the windowsill. Children add a poem as they find one they especially like. Their own poems go in the journal as well. Some enjoy illustrating their journals.

We set aside several weeks when we fill the room with poetry books to heighten awareness about the variety of poems and poets. Reading time is devoted to reading poems, selecting favorites, and copying them in the journals. Browsing through poetry books and reading through poems engages students as they find favorites and read them aloud to a friend. Kelsey copied over thirty-five poems into her poetry journal. Jonathan copied "Sick" (Silverstein 1974b). By the time he had finished, the poem was memorized. He pleased his entire family when he recited it at the Passover dinner. Two years later he liked to stop by the classroom and recite it.

Reciting poems is a relaxing, often playful time in the classroom. We say a new poem in unison. We may divide it into parts. We return to poems we already know. Occasionally we use a poem to time ourselves as we get ready for a new activity: "Let's see if we can have our desks ready for math before we finish saying 'Turkey Time'" (Dunn 1990). Children who memorize poems easily keep the more timid moving along.

When Georgia Heard was working with Lucy McCormick Calkins

at Teachers' College, she gave us new ideas about choral reading, which can pick up student energy on a tired day. As Halloween fever is riding high, choral reading with Halloween poems helps to keep everyone on task. We duplicate ten or twelve poems for everyone. Students choose partners and follow steps that we write on the board:

Choral Reading Performance

1. Browse through the poems.
2. Decide which one to perform.
3. Decide how to recite it.
4. Practice, practice.
5. Perform for the class

After we pass out the sheets of poems, students get into small groups. We circulate to see how each group is doing. In about fifteen minutes, most groups are ready to perform. We pull chairs into two rows to create a stage, and we're ready to begin.

Poetry brings reluctant readers and the printed page together. Short poems are less intimidating than stories. Children who struggle with patterns in reading are supported by repetition and rhyme. For many children, reading and learning poetry are ways to feel successful as they connect literature to their lives.

Poetry is well suited to seven- and eight-year-olds. We marvel at how each class has its own personality. Jane remembers the year Eve Merriam's poems from *You Be Good & I'll Be Night* (1988) electrified her classroom and became chants oft-repeated at unexpected moments. "Hunter on the horse, fox on the run, train leaves the station at one oh one," the children chanted with exaggerated rhythm and voices. When she shared these same poems with the following year's students, they listened attentively, but were not captivated in the same way. Each year the emphasis and interest have their own equation. A curriculum responsive to the students is shaped by them as they interact with it. The organic nature of the curriculum permits the same themes and activities to take on individual flavors as students respond in a variety of ways. The beacon of poetry lights our way as each of us connects our own emotions to the living and learning in the classroom.

Donna's journal reads:

I remember the day in 1953 when I received my first book in the mail from a book club. It was the first chapter book that belonged just to me. I went down in the basement, usually a scary place with imagined monsters lurking in the dark recesses. But that afternoon I settled into the crook of a large drain pipe and read. I left behind my four noisy sisters upstairs and the spooky basement. The author pulled me into the book and I entered into another life. I still can feel the magic of that experience. I had been a solid, top group reader in the school basals. But with that first chapter book, I truly became a reader. I slipped through the white spaces and between the letters and became the spectator in somebody else's life.

When Sara [Donna's daughter] was in second grade, she reported a similar experience. The class had lined up for gym while she sat thoroughly absorbed in a book. As she told me about the story and how she had become totally unaware of her busy classroom, I felt a rush of joy. Sara was a reader! She could forget about individual letters and words on the page and create images and meaning. She could make the book come alive in her imagination. She, too, was hooked.

We celebrate when we find Jaryd in the corner so absorbed in *Babe the Gallant Pig* (King-Smith 1985) that he didn't know it was time for lunch. Or when Derek chatters all the way down the hall about *My Father's Dragon* (Gannett 1948), telling us what happened to Elmer when he saved the baby dragon. We know the indescribable pleasure of being so caught up in a book that we run the risk of missing the boarding call for our flight. Yes, that is our wish for all our students—that reading is not a subject taught in school, but a lifelong habit of wonder and discovery.

References
Abercrombie, Barbara. 1990. *Charlie Anderson*. New York: M. K. McElderry Books.
Baum, Frank L. 1987. *The Wonderful Wizard of Oz*. New York: William Morrow.
Blume, Judy 1976. *Tales of a Fourth Grade Nothing*. New York: Dell.
———. 1980. *Superfudge*. New York: Dutton.
Carlson, Nancy L. 1983. *Loudmouth George and the Sixth Grade Bully*. Minneapolis, MN: Carolrhoda Books.
Cleary, Beverly. 1990. *The Mouse and the Motorcycle*. New York: Avon.
———. 1991a. *Muggie Maggie*. New York: Avon
———. 1991b. *Runaway Ralph*. New York: Avon.
Cole, Joanna. 1990. *The Magic School Bus Lost in the Solar System*. New York: Scholastic.

Dahl, Roald. 1988. *Fantastic Mr. Fox*. New York: Puffin Books.

Davidson, Margaret. 1991. *Louis Braille: The Boy Who Invented Books for the Blind*. New York: Scholastic.

Donnelly, Judy. 1988. *Tut's Mummy Lost—and Found*. New York: Random House.

Drinkwater, John. 1989. "Snail." In *Eric Carle's Animals Animals*. New York: Scholastic.

Dunn, Sonja. 1990. "Turkey Time." In *Crackers & Crumbs*. Portsmouth, NH: Heinemann.

Erickson, Russell. 1993. *A Toad for Tuesday*. New York: Morrow.

Gannett, Ruth Stiles. 1963. *The Dragon of Blueland*. New York: Knopf.

———. 1987a. *Elmer and the Dragon*. New York: Knopf.

———. 1987b. *My Father's Dragon*. New York: Knopf.

Herford, Oliver. 1988. "I Heard a Bird Sing." In *Sing a Song of Popcorn*, edited by Beatrice Schenk de Regniers. New York: Scholastic.

King-Smith, Dick. 1985. *Babe the Gallant Pig*. New York: Crown.

Leverich, Katherine. 1989. *Best Enemies*. New York: Greenwillow.

———. 1991. *Best Enemies, Again*. New York: Greenwillow.

Lowry, Lois. 1988. *All About Sam*. Boston: Houghton Mifflin.

McCloskey, Robert. 1976. *Homer Price*. New York: Puffin.

Merriam, Eve. 1988. *You Be Good & I'll Be Night*. New York: Morrow Junior Books.

Milne, A. A. 1992. *Winnie the Pooh*. New York: Puffin.

Sachar, Louis. 1990. *The Sideways Stories of Wayside School*. New York: Random.

Silverstein, Shel. 1974a. "Boa Constrictor." In *Where the Sidewalk Ends*. New York: Harper & Row.

———. 1974b. "Sick." In *Where the Sidewalk Ends*. New York: Harper & Row.

Smith, Janice Lee. 1988. *The Show-and-Tell War: And Other Stories about Adam Joshua*. New York: Harper & Row.

Verne, Jules. 1962. *Twenty Thousand Leagues Under the Sea*. New York: Macmillan.

Wilder, Laura Ingalls. 1953. *Little House in the Big Woods*. New York: Harper & Row.

The Writing Habit 6

ða "I feel like a real author," said Nathan, "but I'm not as good as Cynthia Rylant yet." Children have a heady feeling during writing workshop because they are in control and doing something they love. As Mike, who was writing the story of his family trip to Egypt, explained, "We'd like to do this all day." Their pores are open to learn new ideas and try out new strategies.

Reading and writing are flip sides of the same coin. Both rely on language and creating mental images. Both depend on the reader or the writer to construct meaning. Both require practice and experience to become more fluent. Both deepen and take on new dimensions when they are discussed and shared. It amazes us that we did not understand the inseparable relationship between reading and writing for the first fifteen years of our teaching. Like many other educators, we thought in terms of separate subjects. We thought the reading/writing connection was having students write about the books they read. Now we observe how being a writer supports and helps the young reader and how a child learns about writing from the stories that are heard and read.

The literature we read to our classes each day becomes our writing text. When we illuminate the craft of James Marshall, Tomie de Paola, Cynthia Rylant, and others, we are explicit about what makes fine writing, humorous stories, or an interesting story line. Book conversations offer information to young writers about how to write a good story. Discussions during reading enrich the writing soil. We point out to students that often we aren't sure whether we are teaching reading or writing since they are so finely meshed. We want children to see a book as a piece of writing that has been crafted by another writer and that has traveled through a predictable writing process before it reached the hands of the reader.

Our own shift in classroom practices began with writing when we were introduced to the work of Don Graves, Lucy McCormick Calkins, Mary Ellen Giacobbe, and Nancie Atwell. In the mid 1980s the district writing curriculum was saturated with story starters and poetry prompts. Sadly absent from writing classrooms were the creativity and excitement we felt in our adult writing group as we struggled to tell our own stories from childhood. The words of Graves and Calkins offered new insights and beginnings. Like a newborn calf on wobbly legs, we took our first steps toward inviting young students into the world of full-fledged authoring. Their overwhelming response to writing workshop signaled its suitability.

We have not stopped learning or coasted serenely among orthodoxies since that time. Quite the contrary. We learned from our distant mentors that we have embarked on a journey without end. And it has become a memorable trip full of new ideas to try, new precepts to formulate, and great conversations with fellow learners, both young and old.

Much has already been written about writing process and writing workshop. The next two chapters give an overview of our writing program, the benchmarks we have noted with our second graders, rituals that infuse writing into all curriculum areas, and the mentoring program we have with classes in other grades.

Writing workshop begins the first day of school. Its independent nature and the choices it offers are the perfect antidote for weary second graders on that long warm afternoon. We keep our introduction to writing workshop brief because sitting and listening abilities are down to a small window of time. Most of our students are familiar with the format of writing workshop, but we review the rules with them. Our large chart reads,

Rules for Writing Workshop

1. Use a quiet voice.
2. Work hard.
3. Don't worry about spelling on drafts.

The first day our goal is to get everyone started on an individual topic. We share several ideas we are considering for our own writing and ask who else has an idea for a story. Evan is anxious to write about his visit to his grandparents in Florida. David thinks about soccer and the excitement of being on a winning team. Sara ponders a story about beach camp and Rachel would like to write about her move to the suburbs from New York City.

After several children have shared story topics, the energy spreads and they are ready to print a title page and take off. A lot is invested in title pages and working on them usually comes first for seven- and eight-year-olds. Some may use this drawing time to rehearse what they are going to say, but for most it is more ritualized—a finished title page is a necessary first step and not much thought is given to what will be said next. To a second grader, a topic and a title are one and the same. When stuck for a story, they say, "I don't have a title." Perhaps that is why the title page can warrant so much attention.

Writing workshop meets the needs of students on that first long and demanding day while it is an excellent early diagnostic time for teachers. Stopping by to confer with each young writer helps us to see where they are developmentally. The personality of each child is subtly exposed as they unself-consciously work on their first piece. Jonathan was drawing pictures of a ninja. He wasn't ready to write with words. Dee Dee bent her head over her stapled booklet and wrote word after word about her vacation in California. Only she could decipher the words, but she wrote with confidence and flair. Scotty started a story like one his older brother had written in second grade, rushing through each word regardless of spacing or letter shapes. Jennifer sat next to him carefully printing a story about a goat her family had to give away because it chewed everything it could get its teeth into. Meredith wrote at the speed of a laser printer and was proud to be the first writer to share her story at the end of the workshop. As a student new to the school, the spotlight of the author's chair gave her reassuring recognition with her classmates.

As we talk with children that first afternoon, we use our own writing as a reference point. We want our students to know that we work hard at writing. Authors of all ages find it comforting to know other writers encounter similar stumbling blocks. When Walt stared off into space after several sentences, Donna recognized the same deep thinking that she experienced at her computer. She bent down next to Walt and chatted quietly with him. Their conversation was not student to teacher but experienced writer to novice. That stance brings a genuine tone and helps students take their own writing more seriously. We keep in mind that we are teaching the writer, not the piece of writing. The individual piece at hand may get buried in a messy folder, but the strategies and skills that fuel writers are hopefully stored and catalogued for continued use.

The range of abilities among second-grade writers is vast. Pearson still preferred to tell his stories pictorially. Liz wrote with a strong voice about best friends, complete with dialogue and detailed passages. In a writing workshop, both can work hard and feel their best effort is appreciated. Both can develop their writing abilities with a sense of satisfaction and pride. Within this landscape of different developmental levels are twenty-three other writers with their own abilities and idiosyncracies. Like all writers, they learn from experience and we plan to give them opportunities to write their own stories at least four times a week. Regardless of present capabilities, we organize the writing time so it is a low-risk and high-learning situation. Children start wherever they are and go from there.

We are patient with writers because we, too, wrestle with getting our thoughts down on paper. We also understand the developmental nature of writing at this grade level, an understanding that lets us view individual writers along the growth continuum rather than imposing the notions of the deficit model so prevalent in earlier writing programs. Peter is spending much of his writing time drawing illustrations and labels each picture with words that confuse most vowels. He has yet to move to the stage of writing where text replaces illustration. Our wish that Peter be a more accomplished writer will not make it so. He needs time, experience, and guidance to grow into the next stage of his development. In a classroom culture permeated with fine literature and alive with writers hard at work, Peter's prognosis is good. We can celebrate each small step he takes as a writer and be there to teach and coax him along the way, with our focus held firmly on what he *can* do.

Myra Barrs illuminates the developmental thinking of six- and seven-year-olds as they decide whether to tell their story through drawing or through writing: "Possibly because drawing is technically easier for them, but possibly too because drawing seems to them superior as a means of expression . . . it may be helpful to consider what it is that some children can do through drawing that cannot be done through writing" (1988, 63). Sensitive educators like Barrs remind us to value the drawing stage of learning to write and not to diminish it in our rush to help our students become authors.

Michael wrote three volumes of *Michael's Inventions*. He gave a great deal of thought to each of his inventions, which displayed his sense of humor as well as his talent in art (see Figure 6-1). His book is an illustrated list, but it is a very sophisticated combination of art and humor. Jane showed Michael *Fantastic Toys* (Beisner 1975), which he enjoyed reading. He had never seen this book before. The writing idea for *Michael's Inventions* had come from his own thinking. To

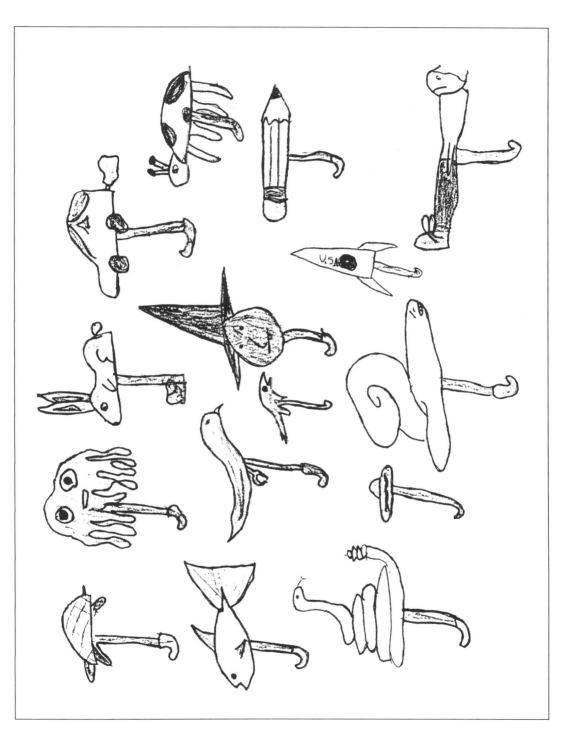

FIGURE 6–1   Michael's Umbrellas

demand written stories from Michael at this stage would negate and diminish his success at storytelling through drawing.

Improving as a writer is not a neat progression along a continuum of development. Each story will not necessarily be better than the one before. If writing were so linear, we could all be Toni Morrison by the time we left freshman English. Like the writing process itself, becoming a better writer is a recursive and uneven proposition, so the growth of a writer needs to be gauged over time. We will talk about portfolio and student reflection, both integral parts of our writing program, in Chapter 7.

Our Writing Workshop

We schedule writing four periods a week. Students look forward to working on their stories and often think ahead to what they will do next, a predictability that enables commitment by writers. The format of workshop time has regular patterns. Students gather in the meeting place for a brief introduction to the workshop or a minilesson. We touch base with everyone by taking status-of-the-class. Children have about thirty to forty minutes to work and confer about their writing. We conclude by meeting on the rug again for group share. The pattern may vary if we have a number of children anxious to read their stories for the class. We may begin and end with a group share or a small group of children may act as a response group to help each other while the rest of the class writes. Most days, however, second graders like to know they can count on the predictable timetable of writing workshop.

Minilessons

Minilessons are just the right size for second-grade listeners anxious to get to their own writing. They take the same daily format. Once we are settled on the rug, we offer a brief word of writer's advice based upon a sense of what is needed. Minilessons can be divided into two broad groups: those that focus on the *procedures* of writing workshop and those that illuminate the *author's craft*. Procedural lessons early in the year ensure that all students know what to expect and what is expected of them. As new ideas emerge or problems develop later on, these lessons help young writers expand their strategies. Procedural lessons include:

- sources of writing ideas
- materials for writing workshop
- keeping and using folders

- what to do with old pieces
- keeping a notebook of writing ideas
- record keeping and story rating
- getting help when you're stuck
- revising
    adding text (spider legs)
    cutting and pasting
    moving text
    changing story sequence
- editing
    personal
    peer
    teacher
- publishing
    why publish
    how to publish
    when to publish
    publishing standards
- status-of-the-class
- writing strategies
    rereading a piece
    rehearsal
    rewriting
    asking questions
- conferring
    role-playing conferences
    conferring questions

Lessons that illuminate the craft of the writer take more time than procedural ones. We may refer to a book we read aloud earlier in the day to highlight a quality of good writing. Here, Jane has reread part of *Mufaro's Beautiful Daughters* (Steptoe 1987) and then asked everyone to listen for the use of beautiful language.

HALLIE: I remember the words *piercing cries*. That scared me a little.

JANE: Those are powerful words.

DAVID: I heard the word *bountiful*, but I am not sure what it means.

JANE: Let's read the sentence again. "She always sang as she worked, and some said it was her singing that made her crops more bountiful than anyone else's." [*Discussion of the word followed.*]

VANESSA: I remember Mufaro "beamed with pride." I've heard those words before.

Jane encourages students to try special language in their own writing. Anyone who uses beautiful language in personal writing that day is invited to bring it to share at the end of writing workshop. Lessons on the author's craft include:

- beautiful language
- information about a subject
- characterization
- setting
- problem/solution
- details
- illustrations
- humor
- leads
- endings
- story sequence
- story flow
- foreshadowing
- alliteration and other patterns
- word variety
- voice
- audience
- inference

When we teach about the craft of writing, we stress a concept over several lessons but don't expect to see results immediately. This instruction offers an invitation to students ready to incorporate the ideas into their writing.

Status-of-the-Class
We keep class lists on a clipboard to use for status-of-the-class. For the first several weeks of school we go down the class list at the end of the minilesson and ask each child about daily work plans. We remind children that this is a good time to listen for writing ideas. What previously was written in our journal becomes known to everyone as all voices are heard. If listening to each others' plans seems to wane, we change the question. A new question keeps this activity from becoming rote. We may ask each class member:

- Who is the main character in your story?
- What is the setting of your story?
- Where did you get the idea for your story?

- Is your work today fiction or nonfiction?
- How long have you been working on this piece of writing?

These are questions we might ask during a conference but using them during status-of-the-class keeps students in touch with what other writers are doing.

Last winter the tight schedule from so many snow days cut into writing time. A number of children needed group share, so Donna didn't take the status-of-the-class for several days. Tommy came over to her during writing and said, "Could you go through the class list the next time we start writing? I want to know what everyone else is doing."

Group Share

The group share time has positive effects upon student writing. As we talk with students at the end of the year about what helps them as writers, group share is mentioned over and over again. It is the time when they are thinking as readers and writers, bringing their knowledge of story and fine writing to the fore, and stating explicitly what it is that makes writing work. When students offer their opinion, they demonstrate their understanding of how words go together to tell a tale or give interesting information.

Children enjoy the limelight. We have a sign-up sheet on the board and they add their names to a list when they wish to share a piece of writing. At the beginning of writers' workshop we check to see if the next two or three students will be ready to share that day.

Second graders can give their undivided attention to two or three stories at a time. As writers begin composing longer stories, we may have only one share so the author can have the full attention of the group. We ask our students to practice reading their piece of writing out loud before they share it with the class, which helps the reading go more smoothly and makes it easier to maintain the interest of classmates. The young author begins the share by telling us how we can help; perhaps the writer needs to think of an ending or perhaps has finished and wants feedback.

The more we share stories, the more we find it a requirement for developing writers. For students who share, hearing their words out loud and sensing the reaction of the group gives another perspective. This activity is too important to be lost in the bustle of the busy day, so we set a timer to signal when the class needs to stop for group share. In his essay *On the Teaching of Creative Writing*, Wallace Stegner stated,

"Merely having a story read aloud and discussed makes it, in the author's eyes, more serious and more worthy" (1988, 63).

Watching Jennifer's proud face as she settled herself on Jane's desk chair speaks to the importance of a time to be heard. Addison's thoughtful comment after her story reminds us that giving students time to talk about each other's writing in the whole group setting deserves to be a priority. Group share holds a magnifying glass to student thinking as we listen to comments and suggestions for the featured writer (see more about group shares in Chapter 8).

Several times a year we have a larger, more public group share. We invite another class to hear our stories or send invitations home to parents to join us for a celebration of our hard work. Last June a class mother baked a special cake in the shape of an open book with the name of every author in the class written with white icing. Each child-author felt individually recognized.

Peer Conferences

One way to improve as a writer is to listen to other writers and to talk with them. Peer conferences elevate young authors to the role of coach and writing critic. As foreign as this may have seemed a decade ago, we now find it age-appropriate and wise to help second graders assume this role. Conferring is integrated into writing workshop as we invite students to read their work aloud to each other for pleasure and feedback.

A young listener may shrug off the responsibility of a peer conference with a quick "Yeah, that was good." We work during share time and in small groups to help children understand and accept the important roles of coach and critic. One of our reference charts reminds everyone how to phrase their comments in gentle ways:

How to Help Another Writer by Conferring
- Tell back what you heard.
- Tell parts that you could really imagine or see.
- Tell parts you would like to hear more about.

As two young authors lean against the wall in the book corner, Jennifer says to Margaret, "How do you want me to help you with your story?" Margaret says, "Just listen to it. I'm not done yet, but I want to know if you like it so far." "OK," says Jennifer.

Margaret then reads her story aloud while Jennifer listens. Margaret looks up when she finishes. Margaret is a friend and Jennifer wants to keep the friendship. She also knows Margaret's story has some gaps.

The responses we use in group share help Jennifer talk in a helpful way to Margaret, so she says, "First, let me tell it back." Jennifer then summarizes the story. Margaret interrupts to correct her, realizing she didn't write what she had wanted. She had left some parts out. Jennifer helps her add them to the story.

Writers of all ages are sensitive about the response their writing receives. In group share we model consideration for feelings and thoughtful comments that can help the writer improve. We teach students that writers must change their mind and not just the text. An author should not be asked to change the text if the author hasn't changed feelings for a story idea. Suggestions from other writers are just that: suggestions, not mandates.

Student-Teacher Conferences

As the senior writers in our rooms, we resist pushing our own wonderful story ideas on fragile and less-mature writers. While it may be difficult to walk away from a story that could be perfected by adult words of wisdom, young writers who insist they like their story the way it is are protecting their expanding sense of authorship.

Talking with young writers about their work in a way that encourages growth as a writer and leaves them eager to continue practicing the craft requires concentration and practice. Lucy McCormick Calkins helped us realize that our primary task was to become a focused listener. After listening and letting the student know what we have heard, we decide what to say during that teachable moment. The conferring model—moving around the room at random, sitting down at eye level with a child, and inviting students to share their stories—creates a workshop atmosphere conducive to sustained writing.

Each quiet conversation with students adds another layer to our understanding of them as writers. Some of the lessons are profound. One afternoon during writing workshop, Ben talked with Donna about his short piece of writing. It was about a pipe rat who lived under an abandoned bathtub. It began, "Somewhere in a time that's been, somewhere on earth, there lived a small pipe rat." The lilt to his language and his imagination were enchanting. Ben had misspelled many of the words and Donna wanted to use his story in a staff development workshop to demonstrate how surface errors can sometimes mask lovely prose. Ben agreed that she could make a copy to share with teachers.

The next day when Donna returned his story, Ben looked her in the eye. "Please, Mrs. Skolnick," he said, "would you tell me what I did right in my story so I can do it again?" His question took her by surprise. Of course, she realized. If we help children know what they do right, they can do it again. Students continue to be our best teachers.

Revision

There was a time when we assumed that a good writing conference with a student led to revision. We thought they would reconsider the story and make improvements based on our conversation. We have altered our expectations as we have grown in our knowledge of second-grade authors.

Revision is a low priority for most seven- and eight-year-olds. Early in the year, going back and reconsidering a story holds little appeal. More mature writers may be willing to opt for small changes but they are the exception. Most of our students find satisfaction in the act of composing and their sense of accomplishment soars when the last page is reached. The big "THE END" at the bottom of the page means just that. They are done.

Revision may take place as the story is being typed for publication, especially if some time has passed. Distance from the writing gives the author a better perspective; sometimes making changes can even be enjoyable. Kat spent several writing periods typing her skiing story onto the computer and was delighted with the changes that now seemed obvious. "I've made this so much better," she told Jane. "I'd left out whole parts before." Kat got fresh ideas when she saw her words on the computer screen.

There are three basic ways a writer can revise a text. The simplest way is to delete text. Second graders prize each word that goes into their story, so this type of revision is rarely a consideration. When Rachel realized she had written "The land was made of candy" in two places, she didn't mind lining it out in one spot. But not all writers can be so realistic or self-critical.

The second way to revise is to move text around or change words. Occasionally students will realize their story is out of order and will rearrange the sentences or pages. Changing individual words is seldom done unless carefully suggested either by a peer or a teacher. For most children the way the original words spilled onto the paper is the way they are meant to be and that order is sacrosanct.

A third way to revise is to add text. This type of revision is the most acceptable to second graders. They love the idea of adding "spider legs" (long strips of paper taped on the side with additional text added) or another page.

In September Mindy was working on a story about what she did in the summer with her sister. "I'm almost finished with my story," she announced. "I only have three more pages to go." Mindy clearly believed that the number of pages in the prepared book dictated the content of her story. Her piece was more of an elaborated list than a story, and she enjoyed adding episodes until she could write "The End" on the last page. Mindy's sense of story is still developing as is her sense of herself as an author. As she gains experience and sophistication as a reader and writer, she will take more control over her story and realize that the story itself determines the length, not the number of pages stapled together in a prepared blank book.

Christy continued adding to her story *The Book About Me* following suggestions made by friends. The piece was transformed into something much more interesting. Especially when there is an adult typist, the active seven-year-old imagination can continue spinning out adventure after adventure as Alison did with her *Halloween Mystery*. Relieved of the burden of needing to copy over, she was more than willing to add to her original story. When Leah's mom acted as typist, her new ideas began to flow.

The ability to revise text changes as the year progresses. Individual patterns emerge as writers realize there is a deep well of language from which to draw. It is a step forward when the young writer decides to improve a story through revision. Several more experienced writers who explain their revisions for a minilesson can spur on classmates to rethink and revise their writing.

Editing

Editing skills require direct instruction and practice. Lessons on the overhead projector focus on one aspect of editing at a time. By the end of second grade we hope all our students are able to edit for capitals, periods, question marks, and conventional spelling. A reference chart on the wall reminds everyone of editing expectations.

Editing is a necessary step before publication. Papers and stories that lie dormant and abandoned in the writing folder do not meet the editing pens. Practice in rereading and editing for a real audience adds a sense of purpose to the task. We don't ask students to edit as an exercise because it is tedious and demanding for a seven year old. First-draft writing may lack proper punctuation and capitalization, but going back to the text after it is declared finished and polishing it for publication eliminates most problems. A basket of editing pens sits with other

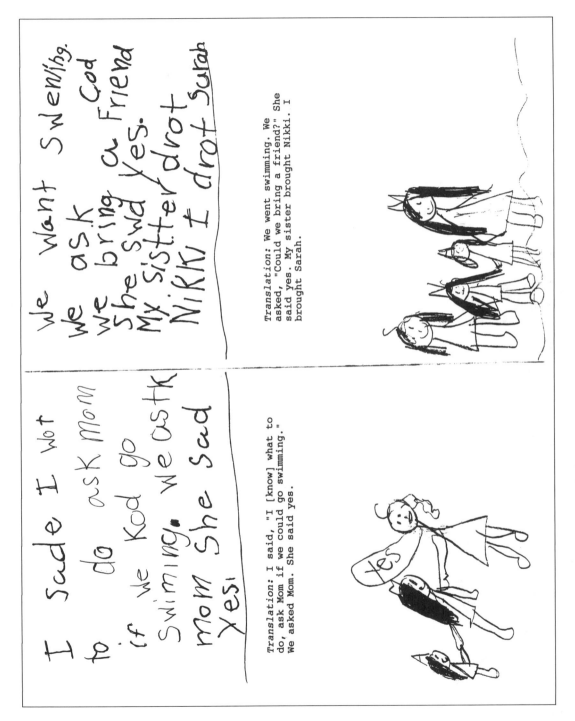

I sade I wot
to do ask mom
if we kod go
swiming. We astk
mom She sad
Yes.

Translation: I said, "I [know] what to do, ask Mom if we could go swimming." We asked Mom. She said yes.

We went Swenlbg.
We ask. Cod
we bring a Friend
She swd yes.
My sistter drot
Nikki I drot Surah

Translation: We went swimming. We asked, "Could we bring a friend?" She said yes. My sister brought Nikki. I brought Sarah.

FIGURE 6-2 Two Pages from Mindy's Story

writing materials, which are used for finished first-draft pieces that are going on to publication. These special green and purple pens appeal to second graders and make the task less arduous.

Sometimes working with an editing partner lightens the job. Some people excel at editing while others seem almost blind to their own errors. We encourage students to do their best as they edit but we are realistic. When the story is typed on the computer by a parent volunteer, further editing takes place as all the spelling and punctuation is made as perfect as possible.

Publishing

Publishing brings with it a more formal recognition of a child's accomplishments as a writer. After a story is typed into book form, the author illustrates the pages using crayons, markers, colored pencils, or a regular pencil. The book is celebrated at group share and a copy goes into the class collection of books. We talk as a class about what the criteria should be for publication.

Not all stories children write become published. Occasionally there is a student like Lars who prefers not to have a prized story typed and spiral bound. He had worked for several weeks on a story about his family vacation, slowly sounding out each word. When we talked about his finished story, he sparkled with pride. He had never sustained a writing effort for so many days or written such a long story. He knew he had expanded his own writing boundaries. Lars looked down at the misspelled, smudged book he held in his hands. "No," he said to Jane's offer to publish it. "I like it just the way it is." The teacher inside Jane wanted to polish up his text and add it to the class library, but the writer in her understood his feelings. A clean, typed copy would gloss over all the hard work and erase the days of effort. Lars had not written the story because it was assigned or to put it in the book corner. He had written it for himself. It had been a challenging and satisfying experience. When he read his story for the writing celebration, he read from his original copy and it was just as impressive.

A published story can be a real boost for a seven-year-old. For the past several years we have used parent volunteers to help with publishing and we recommend volunteers enthusiastically. We have been fortunate to have one volunteer assisting in a forty-five-minute time slot four days a week. We move the computer and printer into the hall and the parent sits with the author as the story is typed. The volunteers are able to work with one or two writers each session. A sign-up sheet helps us keep track of who is ready for a turn.

Parent volunteers help ensure that the publishing keeps a steady pace. At the beginning of the year we make sure our typists understand that, except for issues of writing conventions, the young authors have final authority over their stories. Parents have been considerate about respecting the language of the writer.

One of the longest-lasting battles Donna fought as a townwide writing teacher was trying to remove the number requirement from the writing guidelines. This battle occurred during the district transition from story starters to allowing children to work through the authoring process. Some administrators felt the only way to ensure productive writing programs was to mandate at least one published piece of writing a month. Removing this requirement signalled an understanding of the twists and turns in many children's developmental paths.

Our goals for young writers have far exceeded an arbitrary number of final pieces collected in a folder. When students think and work like writers, some pieces may take a number of weeks. We have been delighted by the sustained effort students have made on a writing project. The former notion of a quick first draft on an assigned topic followed by teacher editing and student recopying for the folder seems as archaic as the portable typewriters we used in college. With the wide range of abilities in our classrooms, we are learning to encourage rigor and commitment while respecting the complexities and ambiguities of the craft of writing.

Patterns and Characteristics

Leland Jacobs writes the following in the August/September 1987 issue of *Teaching K–8*:

> Teachers may ask: If writing isn't self-expression, then what is it? It is the ordering of thought. It is the forming of an idea, or a cluster of ideas, from a child's experiences and imagination. It is a conscious shaping of the materials selected by the writer to be included in the composition. In selecting what to put in and leave out, the child is using those elements of writing craftsmanship that he or she can manage. In other words, writing is a disciplined act on the part of the writer at his or her level of development. (38)

Second-grade writers demonstrate patterns and problems that reflect their level of development even as their skill levels vary greatly. When school starts in September, the children who come to us range in age from six to eight and a half. Within that age span we anticipate a writing range from drawing to telling stories through complex story lines with dialogue and description. Between these two markers will be a host of other developmental levels.

Illustration as Story
For the children who best tell their stories through drawing, we encourage growth from adding first labels and then—as they seem ready over time—sentences to accompany the pictures. Sean asks as he begins each story, "May I just do pictures?" Donna reassures him that the pictures will lead him to a story. Sean is able to relax, draw his ideas, and then seek the help he needs to write words that tell about the pictures. The effort it takes him to draw a story, compared with the effort it takes him to write his story, is the difference between walking on a sandy beach in the sunshine and walking against the wind in a blinding blizzard. Our primary goal is to encourage Sean to share his thinking on paper and to know that he has stories to tell. We will continue to nudge him but know that asking him to conform to grade-level expectations will be counterproductive. He has his own timetable and we are confident he will grow to be able to tell his story with words.

When children still need to develop their ideas and organize their stories with drawings, we provide the paper and materials to make their art work the best it can be. As we confer with them, we point out ways their drawing can be enhanced through a story line. As our friend and colleague Anne Nesbitt tells her second graders, she is not concerned with whether James Marshall drew his illustrations or wrote his text first. The end result is a delightful meshing of the two. Our students have that same permission.

Making Lists
Second graders love lists and the longer the better. Sometimes partners put their heads together to concoct lists of their favorite things. One small booklet may be favorite flavors of ice cream illustrated with an ice-cream cone on each page that has been colored a shade to match the flavor. Another booklet may be a list of favorite colors. Alex and Casey filled ten pages with "Army Things." They drew and labeled camouflage uniforms and helmets. Lexy wrote her long book *The Little Mermaid*. Before she wrote, she laid out her plans using a list of chapters to organize her writing (see Figure 6-3). Riddle or joke books are another example of list books. A few children actually make up jokes, which is enormously appreciated by the class. When well-known jokes

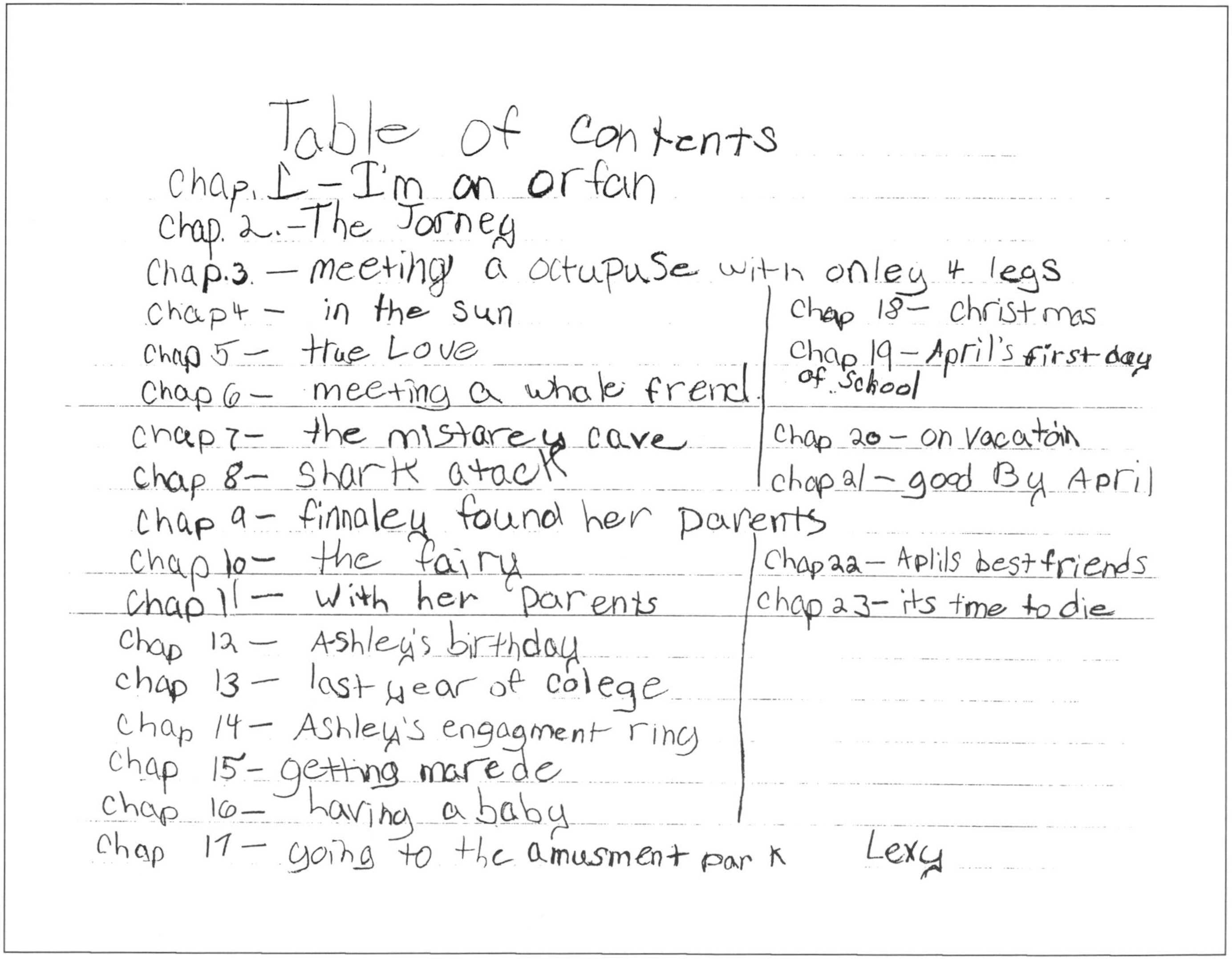

Table of Contents

chap. 1 — I'm an orfan
chap. 2 — The Jorney
chap. 3 — meeting a octupuse with onley 4 legs
chap. 4 — in the sun
chap. 5 — true Love
chap. 6 — meeting a whale freind
chap. 7 — the mistarey cave
chap. 8 — shark atack
chap. 9 — finnaley found her parents
chap. 10 — the fairy
chap. 11 — with her parents
chap. 12 — Ashley's birthday
chap. 13 — last year of colege
chap. 14 — Ashley's engagment ring
chap. 15 — getting marede
chap. 16 — having a baby
chap. 17 — going to the amusment park
chap. 18 — christmas
chap. 19 — April's first day of school
chap. 20 — on vacation
chap. 21 — good By April
chap. 22 — Aplils best friends
chap. 23 — its time to die

Lexy

FIGURE 6–3 Lexy's Plan

are written down or revised, students seem to enjoy hearing them retold by a peer.

To our concrete thinkers, a list is a solid, safe, and fun way to tell about their world. This phase passes into a desire to tell a story, often from their own life experiences.

Personal Narrative

Some students begin second grade ready to tell a story with words. A favorite topic is "All about Me." Sarah began her story this way:

> I lived in Korea when I was a baby. My mom couldn't keep me. She put me on a plane and I have a new family. I got a mommy and a daddy and two dogs. I arrived two days before my first birthday.

This year Colin's first story was a travelogue about his trip to Florida. That gave Henrik the idea to write the story of his family trip to Niagara Falls. Later, Colin wrote about his own trip to Niagara Falls (see Figure 6-4). A travelogue is easier to write than some other genres because the need for a beginning, middle, and end is eliminated by staying with the sequence of events as they happened.

Early Fiction

When writers are ready to move into inventing their own stories, they often begin by telling the story in a progression, much like the time line travelogue. Sentences are hooked together with the words "And then." These bed-to-bed stories are a signature style of second graders. A minilesson on the overhead projector can help students realize that the sentence connectors are not necessary to the meaning of the story. Many young writers continue to use connectors in their rough drafts but are able to take some out when they edit.

Stories with Sequence

The next level is the ability to write a story with a beginning, middle, and end. Discussions about books and their structure help writers organize their own stories. Stories that have a problem for the main characters and end with a solution may follow. However, even with numerous conversation about problems and solutions during reading and writing, some students will be able to recognize these in the writing of classmates or in literature but will not yet be able to construct their own stories on this model.

Mystery stories are especially popular with our students. When

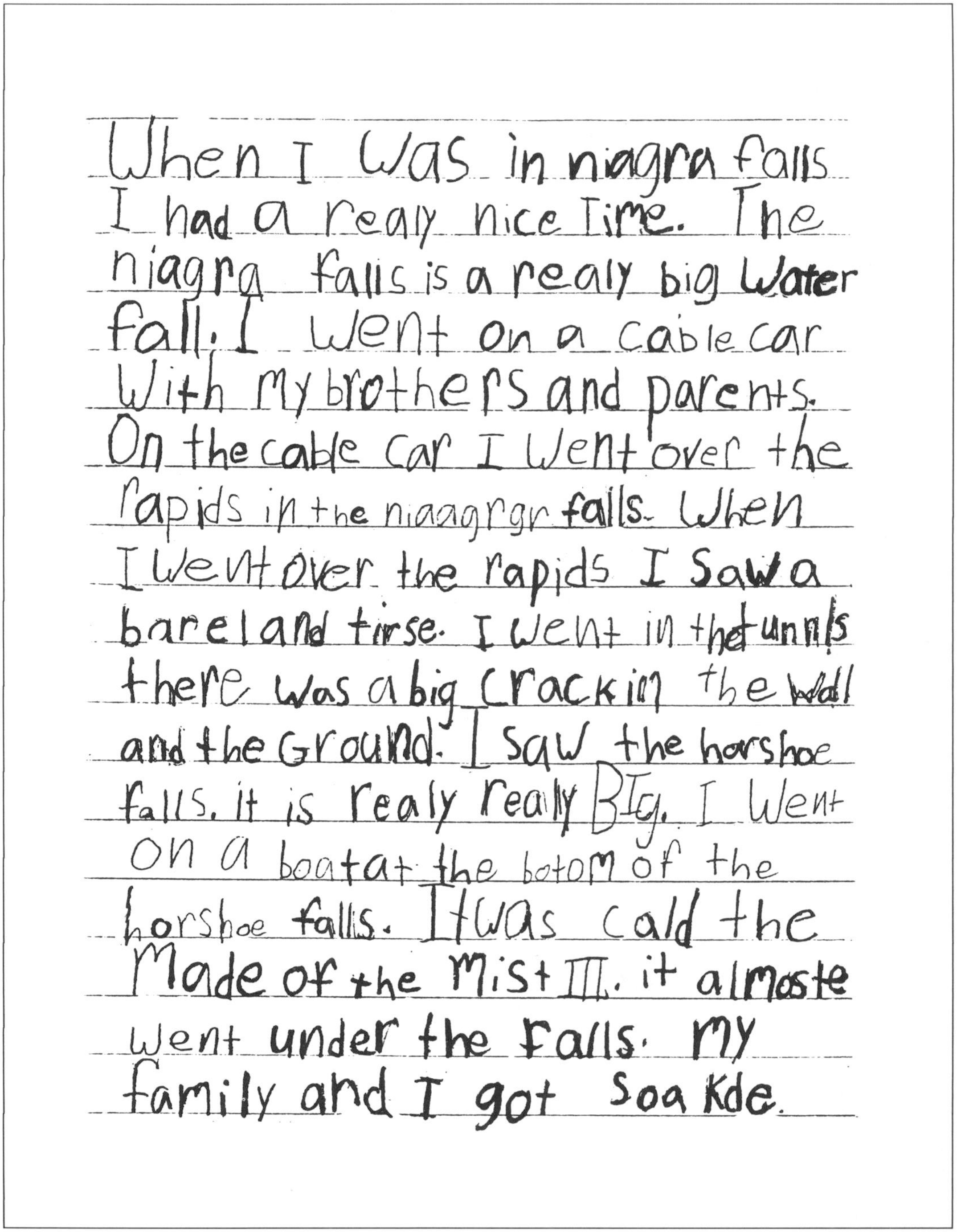

When I was in niagra falls I had a realy nice Time. The niagra falls is a realy big Water fall. I Went on a cable car With my brothers and parents. On the cable car I Went over the rapids in the niaagrgr falls. When I Went over the rapids I Saw a bareland tirse. I Went in the tunnls there was a big crack in the wal and the Ground. I Saw the horshoe falls. it is realy realy BIg. I Went on a boat at the botom of the horshoe falls. It was cald the Made of the Mist III. it almoste Went under the Falls. My family and I got Soakde.

FIGURE 6–4   Page One of Colin's Travelogue

trying to write them, most children become bogged down in the elements that create a good mystery. It is hard to keep the reader in suspense and find a believable solution. Michael wrote *The Mystery of the Disappearing Hannukah Present*. At share time, David told him that the present was obviously under the chair in the illustration. Nathan felt there was no suspense. Michael returned to work on the piece. He pasted a new paper over that page in his book and redrew the picture with the present mostly hidden by discarded wrapping paper. The class approved this revision by clapping for Michael.

Poetry

Some students enjoy writing poetry. Amber wrote her poem "Horrible Dreams," but she couldn't decide how to organize it and where to put in line breaks. Jane photocopied her poem and gave copies to small groups of children who agreed to help Amber. Each group read the poem, discussed its organization, and put slashes on the paper where they thought a line break should occur. The groups read the versions aloud in choral form for Amber and the rest of the class to hear. There were six different suggestions. Next, Jane typed the proposals made by the different groups on a piece of paper and made copies. Everyone enjoyed seeing and reading the differences. After receiving the input of her classmates, Amber wrote the poem in her poetry journal based upon her own decision about where the line breaks should be. Figure 6-5 shows how Amber put the line breaks in her poem before the class helped her. Figure 6-6 is the way she wrote it in her journal.

Naming Characters

Using character names is a mark of more sophistication. Many boys enjoy writing stories about superheroes and will use those types of names or general titles such as "bad guys" or "ninjas." Girls often like to use the names of their friends in stories. As more children decide to use classmates' names in their writing, the group needs to decide if prior approval is necessary. In Meredith's story *The Sleep Over*, her main (female) characters had names but later in the story another character was referred to as "a boy." When Jane asked her why she hadn't given that character a name, Meredith explained that he was not an important character and would only be in the story a little bit.

Dialogue

Another mark of more mature writing is the use of dialogue. Long before they are able to use quotation marks, some students have their

horrible dreams

Sleeping alone in your bed
with horrible dreams dancing
in your head What could it be
dancing in your head While
your sleeping in your bed

FIGURE 6–5   Amber's Draft Showing Possible Line Breaks

Horrible dreams

by Amber.

Sleeping alone in your bed
with horrible dreams dancing in your head
What could it be dancing in your head
while you're sleeping
in your bed.

FIGURE 6–6   Amber's Revised Poem

characters talk. First they may use cartoon-type bubbles to indicate speaking. Next, talk is often written as strings of words without any marks to indicate the actual speech or the speaker, as in Kira's story (Figure 6-7). When students read their stories with dialogue aloud, their inflection and expression gives the listener clues to who's talking. The authors probably hear the distinct voices as they write.

As parents type these stories, they help students understand the use of punctuation and quotation marks. Teaching, through minilessons on the overhead projector, demonstrating with our own writing, or displaying a page from a favorite book with dialogue helps young writers see the purpose of quotation marks. Another technique is reading dialogue aloud like a play (see Chapter 8). As audience awareness grows, children realize the need to help the reader understand who is speaking. Not all second graders reach the point in their writing where they include dialogue, but all can benefit from noticing how authors use dialogue to help the reader know the characters better.

Details

Jane's class was learning about using details in writing and how authors and illustrators use them to enhance a story. Jane read *The Stranger* (van Allsburg 1986) and asked the children to take note of details for discussion after the story.

DAVID: Look at his eyes in the cover picture. He looks astonished.

RACHEL: All the pictures have details. Look at the hand holding the thermometer. Look at the cats. You can almost see each hair of their fur.

NATHAN: Listen to these words: "The steam that rose from the hot food fascinated him." I never heard an author talk about steam from food.

COURTNEY: Here's something else: "Occasionally Mr. Bailey would have to stop and rest. But the stranger never tired. He didn't even sweat." (giggles)

Literature highlights how authors use details to create a special mood or to help the reader create mental imagery. We may make a reference chart to brainstorm the role details can play in writing. Some second graders have a natural flair for details. The story in Figure 6-8 by Gabrielle shows her use of detail to help develop her character. Gabrielle wrote this story late in October, but many classmates may not achieve this level of storytelling until third grade. The more mature

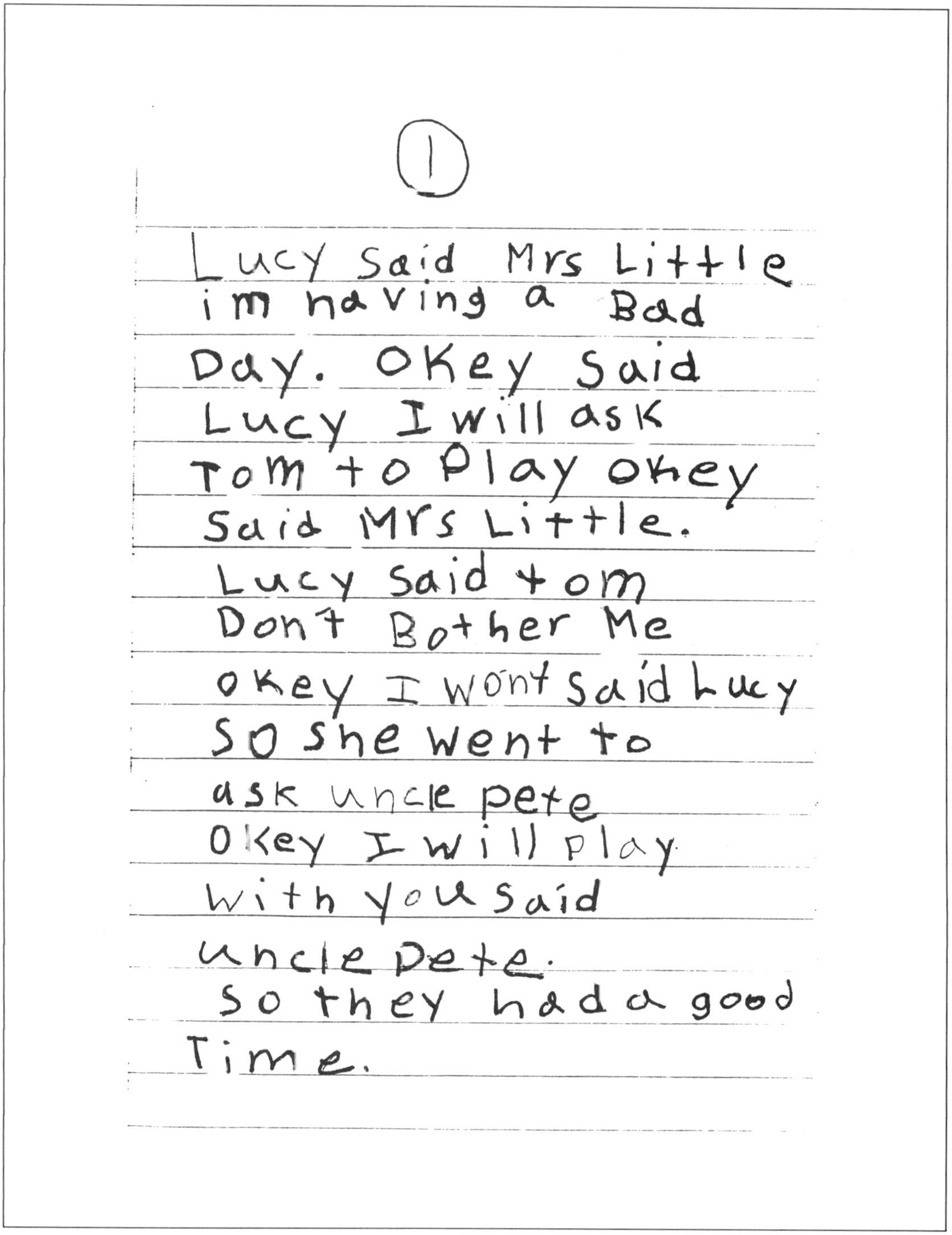

(1)

Lucy said Mrs Little
im having a Bad
Day. Okey said
Lucy I will ask
Tom to Play okey
said Mrs Little.
Lucy said tom
Don't Bother Me
okey I wont said Lucy
So she went to
ask uncle pete
Okey I will play
with you said
uncle pete.
So they had a good
Time.

FIGURE 6-7   Kira's First Draft

(1.)

Owans upan a
time thar livd
a giai and she
lovd the samar
and hatid the winter
she was 9 yers old.
her name was Gab wen it was
the winter she
just Jrak hot
chaklit and ayt
chesdotals wiy waching
tv. And in the
sammar she was
to bisy to do that
stof. she was picing
Apals and planting
flawrs and having
piknins.

FIGURE 6–8   Gabrielle's First Draft

writers blaze the trail and show us where others will follow in their own time.

Audience

Seven- and eight-year-olds are beginning to be aware of audience. Some students write their stories for the reaction they will get from their classmates. Scottie wrote and shared "The Adventures of Sumo and Yosi," two huge Sumo wrestlers who subdue their enemies by sitting on them. Scottie knew his classmates would laugh when he read that part. He was right. The journal Jane kept during her first year back in the classroom says the following about audience:

> When kids talk about their writing it helps me see the growth. Before I knew to ask them questions, I guess I was not as fully aware. I asked them twice about audience, who they wrote for. In February Steven said he doesn't write for anybody, he just writes what comes to his mind. In April he reported that he wrote for his friends. Aoife said she wrote for herself in February, but added in April that she writes because she likes to do it, it's fun. In the first interview Jodi said she didn't know who her audience was, but in April she told me she wrote for Sandra [a much-admired writer in the class].

Awareness of audience is both a plus and a minus. On the positive side, students who realize they are writing for others work harder to make their stories interesting and appealing. But that struggle may have a downside: the same student who happily wrote story after story in first grade without consideration for the approval of others begins to be inhibited by the idea of audience. For uncertain writers, this step forward in awareness may further complicate writing as they worry what classmates might think.

Voice

If we had written about writing workshop six or seven years ago, we would have spent time explaining why it is imperative for children to choose their own topics. An essential part of full-fledged authoring, choice has become a given. Writing about a topic that originates with the child brings their individual voice into the piece.

Prospect and Retrospect by James Britton (1982) helped us understand why. Personal writing lets students be spectators in previous events in their lives. Telling their own stories allows them to retell and reshape their past. Through reshaping and interpreting personal experiences, they find their voices as writers and storytellers. Our task is to safeguard and nurture that voice as we encourage them to write about what matters to them.

When children write from their own lives and interests, they can write with an authority not available to them when the topic has been assigned and is outside their realm of experience. Voice in the writing of a second grader is an exciting quality to find. Jennifer told her story with a style and voice uniquely her own (see Figure 6-9).

There is an energy in this first page that signals her control over her writing. Jennifer is one of the most prolific writers in the class and chooses to write whenever there is a free moment. Her writing reflects all the reading she does.

Often we can tell that a student loves to read by the way that student writes. Rebecca's story imitates the style and voice of John Peterson's *The Littles* books, some of her favorite reading. Written early in the school year, her story is a worthy attempt at writing like Peterson. She uses transitional words such as *meanwhile* and *while*. "She was talking to herself and hoping her family remembered her birthday" follows a language pattern more like the books she reads than that usually found in second-grade writing. Her reading influences her voice as a writer and her choice of subject matter (see Figure 6–10).

Point of View

Point of view is difficult for second-grade writers. Meredith's story *The Sleep Over* is typical of many stories in which the person telling the story switches from third to first person.

> Once upon a time there was a girl named Rachel that was going to have her first sleep-over at her friend's house. Her friend's name is Laura. She is five years old and Rachel is six. . . . [The story progresses as the girls go to an amusement park together.] Then we went home for dinner. We had spaghetti with meatballs. It was homemade. Then we went to sleep.

When Donna talked with Meredith about who was telling the story, she looked confused. Donna tried several ways to help her see that in the beginning the story was written in the third person and then it changed to first person as Meredith herself becomes the storyteller. After several minutes, Meredith decided she liked her story the way it was (see Figure 6-11). The ability to maintain a point of view in writing

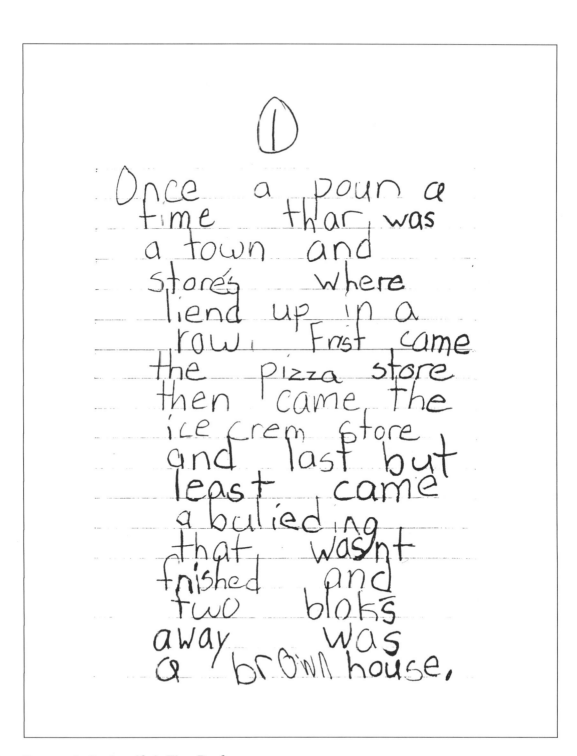

Once a poun a
time thar was
a town and
stores where
liend up in a
row, Frist came
the pizza store
then came the
ice crem store
and last but
least came
a bulied ing
that wasn't
frished and
two bloks
away was
a brown house.

FIGURE 6–9   Jennifer's First Draft

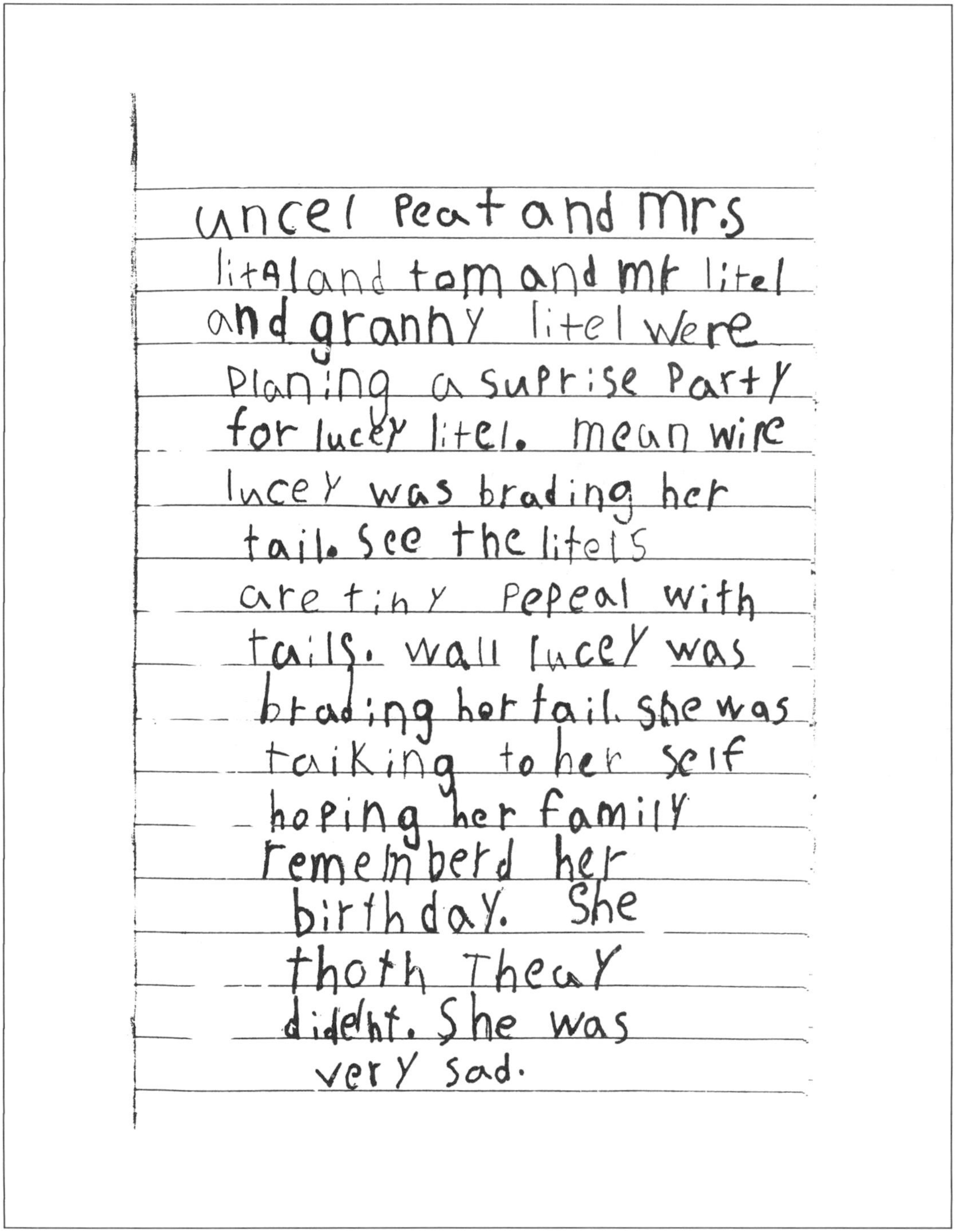

uncel Peat and Mrs.
litaland tom and mr litel
and granny litel were
Planing a suprise Party
for lucey litel. mean wire
lucey was brading her
tail. see the litels
are tiny pepeal with
tails. wall lucey was
brading her tail. she was
taiking to her self
hoping her family
rememberd her
birthday. She
thoth theay
dident. She was
very sad.

FIGURE 6–10 Rebecca's First Draft

resolves itself over time. Until children are able to see the difference between first and third person, they are often reluctant to make changes. We give our students the time they need when they indicate a desire to leave the text as it was originally written.

Tense

A similar but even more complex problem is the tense in a story. Most children happily tell their story as if it happened in the past, which fits easily with the "Once upon a time" mode they've heard repeatedly. Some more experienced writers do grapple with using the appropriate tense. Amy expressed it this way: "I don't know whether it's happening right now or whether I'm telling it from a long time ago." The challenge, as with first and third person, is explaining tense in a way that concrete and transitional thinkers can understand. When they do, we feel quite accomplished. In many instances, however, we again decide to be patient and let maturation take its course. Like pouring pancake batter on a cold griddle, some things just need time before they can be properly cooked and understood. Wallace Stegner again speaks to our experience: "The literary apprenticeship, despite the contrary evidence of certain precocious individuals, is normally long. . . . And the maturing process cannot be taught, it has to happen" (1988, 19).

Children may also use writing workshop time to write a letter, a notice, a play, a puppet show, or a poem. Our guiding question is, Will this help you become a better writer? Is it important to you? Some students need to come to writing through the back door. If a letter to a professional wrestler ignites David's interest, then he drafts and recopies his letter and it goes into the mail. Our job is to help students understand the variety of possible ideas and writing projects. We encourage them to keep thoughts, questions, story fragments, and observations in their writing notebooks to consider later as seeds for full-blown pieces of writing. The door is open and the list is long. We seldom hear students say they don't know what to write.

The decision of topic belongs to each individual. Whatever it is a child decides to work on, we see the patterns and characteristics we have described. Individual differences cover the whole range of writing skills. Some read voraciously and are so deeply affected by published authors that we can see their influence in the student writing. Some read very little and are struggling to find a voice of their own. We work with students on an individual level, hoping to teach them to become more fluent, diverse writers with unique voices.

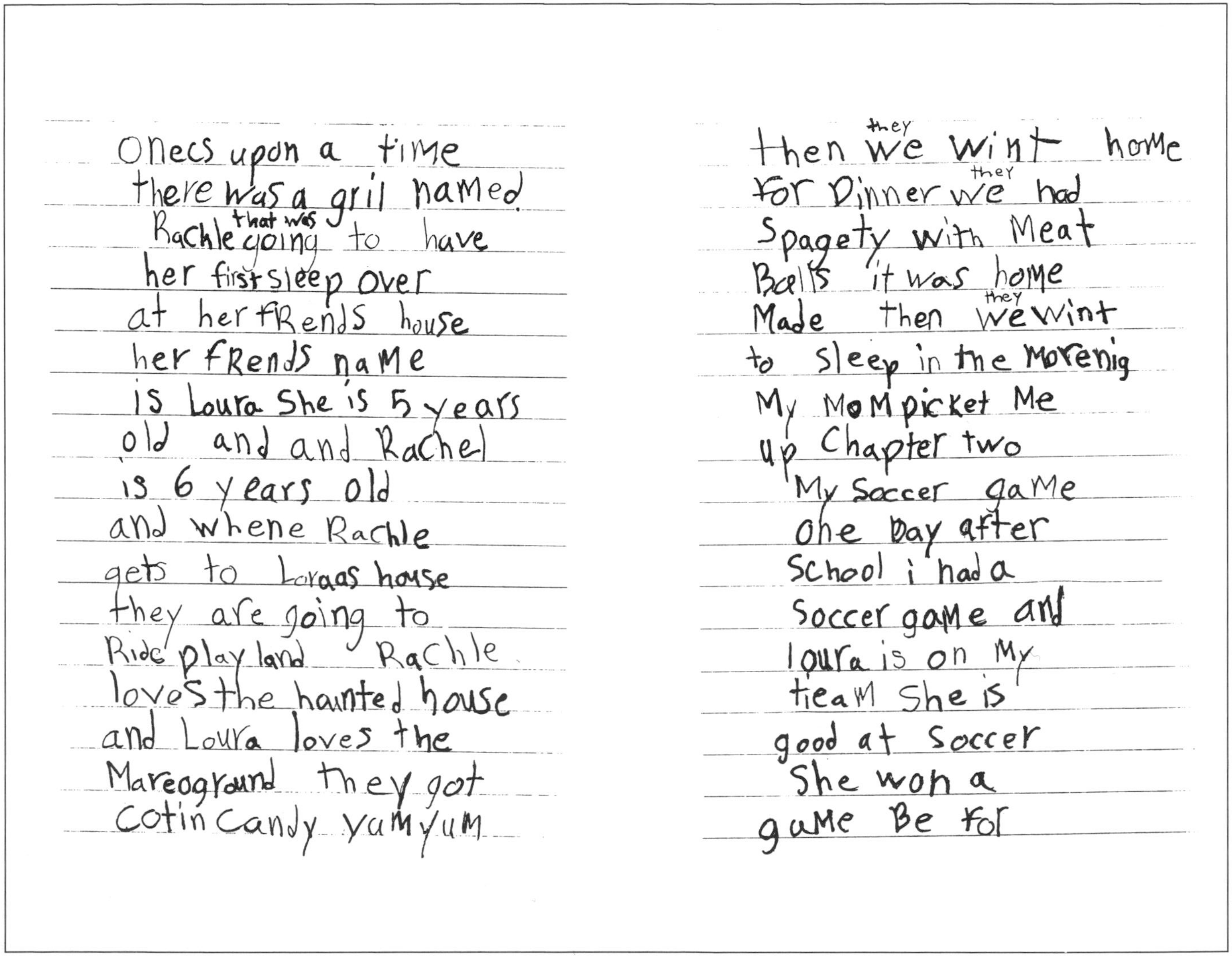

Onecs upon a time
there was a gril named.
Rachle that was going to have
her first sleep over
at her freinds house
her freinds name
is Laura she is 5 years
old and and Rachel
is 6 years old
and whene Rachle
gets to lauras house
they are going to
Ride play land Rachle
loves the haunted house
and Laura loves the
Mareogrand they got
Cotin Candy yum yum

then we wint home
for Dinner we had
spagety with Meat
Balls it was home
Made then we wint
to sleep in the Morenig
My Mom picket Me
up chapter two
My soccer game
one Day after
school i had a
soccer game and
Laura is on My
team she is
good at soccer
she won a
game Be for

FIGURE 6–11 Meredith's First Draft

Wherever each student is on the continuum, writing workshop is a favorite activity. Children are proud of their accomplishments and feel the special energy that comes from making their own decisions and getting recognition for their accomplishments.

References

Barrs, Myra. 1988. "Drawing a Story: Transitions Between Drawing and Writing." *The Word for Teaching Is Learning*, edited by Martin Lightfoot and Nancy Martin. Portsmouth, NH: Heinemann.

Beisner, Monika. 1975. *Fantastic Toys*. Chicago: Follett.

Britton, James. 1982. *Prospect and Retrospect: Selected Essays of James Britton*, edited by Gordon M. Pradl. Portsmouth, NH: Heinemann.

Jacobs, Leland. 1987. "The Child Writer." *Teaching K–8* 18 (August/September): 38.

Peterson, John L. 1977. *The Littles and the Trash Tinies*. New York: Scholastic.

Stegner, Wallace. 1988. *On the Teaching of Creative Writing: Responses to a Series of Questions,* edited by Edward Connery Lathem. Hanover, NH: University Press of New England.

Steptoe, John. 1987. *Mufaro's Beautiful Daughters*. New York: Lothrop, Lee & Shepard.

van Allsburg, Chris. 1986. *The Stranger*. Boston: Houghton Mifflin.

Managing and Extending the Writing Habit

7

&❦ In her new role as a teacher trainer for the writing project, Jane is relearning that teachers feel uncomfortable about their ability to manage a writing or reading workshop if they have never done so before. In practice, managing a workshop is not nearly so difficult as it may look because the students help with the management by their attention to the task and their desire to work on what they enjoy doing. For teachers new to this approach, writing workshop may seem like needing to keep too many balls in the air, an impossible juggling act.

We have devised some ways to keep track of what each student is doing, who needs help, who needs the proverbial nudge, who needs to publish, and so forth. We know that writing workshop works better than our old "writing time" ever did and that students learn more as they take charge of their writing time. Experience has taught us the power of choice and flexibility.

We begin this chapter with some of the organization techniques we have developed since our return to the classroom. They work well, but like everything we do they are in transition, ready to be modified or changed if something better occurs to either us or our students. We continue the chapter with a discussion of writing mentors and conclude with some ideas about writing throughout the day.

Classroom Management

Student activity during writing workshop bears little resemblance to former writing times. We can remember when the writing assignment was explained and children were expected to work quietly at their desks.

Some teachers even prowled up and down the aisles like security guards to be sure students were on task and not talking to each other. Teacher comments included. "You can't write and talk at the same time." The accepted belief was that silence was the mark of a productive writing time.

When our teachers first began inviting their students into full-fledged authoring, we knew we had to help administrators change how they judged a fruitful writing period. One principal visited a second-grade class and wondered why some students were using magic markers during writing. He couldn't understand why they were sitting together and sharing stories. The forced tranquility of former writing times seemed to have given way to quiet chaos. Unfortunately, the principal did not know how to bend down next to students and listen to their stories or talk to them about their writing or he may have revised his initial opinion that students were not on task. He needed help from teachers before he could begin to see the theory behind the practice and to know that the activities allowed in the room had been carefully thought out and orchestrated.

Our role during writing workshop feels much better than the previous role of being a guard at the gate. Writing workshop time flies by as we circulate to coach writers, answer questions, listen to stories, help a student find the right materials, and keep a finger on the pulse of the activity. When the energy level is dropping we know it is time to tell writers that they have two minutes to finish up before group share.

Careful classroom management is one of the cornerstones of a successful writing workshop. Without the rituals and patterns in place, eager second-grade writers can leave their teachers feeling like they are chasing a runaway train. How do we keep up with all the different writers and their work? Some suggestions are mentioned below:

1. We have a space on the board where students sign up for a teacher conference. We know who wants our attention and this list keeps a line from forming behind us like a Chinese dragon.
2. We wear a sign that reads: "Writing conference in progress. Please come back later." It reminds young writers not to interrupt and to be patient; we will hear their piece soon.
3. During each writing workshop, students who feel they have the time and inclination may volunteer to help others. If writers want someone to hear a story right that minute, they can check a list to see who is

willing. Children put their names after the appropriate item on this list on the front board:

I can help with
finding a topic
conferring
editing
writing at the computer
illustrating

4. Some children like to compose or type their stories on the computer. For children with fine-motor delays or difficulties, writing stories on the computer opens a welcome world of possibilities. Collaborating with a friend at the keyboard works well. About midyear Nancy Cort, our computer teacher, introduces the class to the word processing program Magic Slate and then the demand for our one computer soars. Other teachers in the building are generous about letting our students work quietly at the computer in their rooms while their class is doing something else. We reciprocate whenever possible. Our parent volunteers do not come during writing workshop, so the computer is free for students to work on their own stories.

5. There are days when writers need a break and we are happy to let them curl up and be carried away with a good book. Waiting for the muse is more productive in the company of a literary friend.

6. Students keep all their work in a folder with pockets. Student record keeping includes a rating of how well they like each story they have written. A weekly reminder helps to maintain a current record. Students are encouraged to organize their work if they label one side of their folder "Works in Progress" and the other side "Finished Pieces." For many second graders, organization is not a natural skill and they need demonstrations of how to keep their writing together.

7. We set aside time each week to review the work in writing folders. Between this check, regular status-of-the-class questions, and our conferences when we jot brief notes in our journals, we are able to keep up with the dynamic energy that powers writing workshop like a giant turbine.

Mentors

We derive inspiration and fresh ideas from our mentors. Our budding authors need the same kind of mentoring, which we try to provide in a variety of ways. We read aloud from carefully selected picture books.

We read stories we have saved from past second graders and invite older students to visit our classroom to share their writing. We read material that children's authors and illustrators have written about themselves—books such as *A Writer* (Goffstein 1984) and *If You Were a Writer* (Nixon 1988)—and invite "real" authors to speak.

Teachers in our school cooperate so that older writers can serve as mentors for younger ones. Jane scheduled writers' share with Caltha Crowe, who teaches fourth grade. When the fourth-grade students came to room 13—where some of them had been students two years previously—they carried their pieces with them to share with seven- and eight-year-olds.

Jacqueline, Jane's former student, read the story of her February vacation trip to the assembled group. Fourth graders were the first to comment. But soon questions and comments came from second graders as well. It was obvious that the modeling done by the older children influenced the way Jane's students phrased their comments.

Elizabeth, one of Caltha's students, suggested to Jacqueline that she could make the piece more personal. She wanted to know how Jacqueline felt about being in a strange place where people spoke a different language. Jacqueline had written that her mother did not allow her to leave the family group because she was worried about what might happen if Jacqueline had difficulty communicating. Elizabeth wanted Jacqueline to tell her audience how she felt about that. Allison, one of Jane's students, suggested the use of the pronoun *I* rather than *we* to make the story more personal.

Courtney, Jane's student, read a story about her family to the assembled group. Her sister Casey was a student in Caltha's room. Casey laughed when she heard Courtney describe a family party from her point of view. Casey asked her sister to tell everyone what she, Casey, had done with her cousin and suggested Courtney add to her story. Courtney was able to incorporate some of Casey's comments.

Jane and Caltha arranged regular times for sharing together. Students rotated, sometimes going to one classroom, sometimes to the other. When special relationships developed between students in the two rooms, their teachers looked for other ways to let them work together. Jordan came weekly to read with eight-year-old Michael. Jordan modeled for Michael, talked with him about reading strategies, and helped him with fluency. These relationships replicated the natural and positive mentoring that takes place in families.

We wrote about Jane's second graders acting as mentors for children being initiated into writing workshop in Hilda Rhodes's kindergarten in the section on expanded opportunities in Chapter 1. Each class was divided in half so that Hilda and Jane worked with a group composed of half kindergarten and half second-grade students. Children paired up with siblings, friends, and neighbors. Hilda and Jane planned minilessons and writing activities, knowing that the older children would help the younger ones.

Eight-year-old Carlos and five-year-old Derek worked together on their book about pets. Jane noticed a patience and gentle coaching in Carlos that she would not have thought possible of this special-needs student. Hilary assisted Ashley with her writing, refraining from spelling words for her. Hilary helped her listen to the sounds and use inventive spelling as she had learned in kindergarten.

When the groups came to a natural pause in their writing and illustrating, both classes met for a celebration. Popcorn was the usual fare as Hilda played her guitar and the group sang songs. Everyone was riveted as students read a group big book or a piece written by a pair of children. The modeling for questions and comments came from second graders as they inspired the children in kindergarten. A sense of pride linked the children.

Mentoring occurs within a class as well and may be observed at group share or during writing time. Some ideas catch like wildfire once they are introduced by a class member. Jane watched as many versions of ice-cream lists were produced by one class. We overhear Adam suggest to his good friend Jordy that he include a certain story in his memoirs. Ashley and Alison write a book together. They talk over how they will divide the work, what to include, how they will share it with the class, and whether they feel it is worthy of publishing.

Literature is an important source for mentoring. Just as we are influenced by our favorite authors, so our students become aware of how literature impacts upon their writing. We cheer them on as they set their sights on writing like a favorite author. We confess our desire to write like Beverly Cleary, Judy Blume, Sigrid Undset, or Wallace Stegner. Writing is a mental experience that taps into the storehouse of all the books we have read and all the words we have written. Jessica explained her eight-year-old version of the reading-writing connection: "Whether I'm reading or whether I'm writing, I don't know where the story is going. Both are mysteries to me. I like that."

Writing Throughout the Day

Writing is an integral part of the school day. In every curriculum area, it lets our students think on paper, externalizing their thoughts and ideas.

Weekend News

The first day of the week students write and share their weekend news. As the year begins they are able to write, on average, from one sentence to five or six sentences. For many, their main focus is illustration. Writing fluency develops quickly as the children learn that activities with their families and friends are a source of stories rich in detail. Seven- and eight-year-olds begin writing more interesting and complex accounts of activities away from school and take great pleasure in composing interesting weekend news stories. During September and October we use the format shown in Figures 7–1 and 7–2. When writing overtakes the need for illustration our second graders are proud to graduate to journals for their weekend news.

Sean was fascinated by his own ability to write a very detailed account of his weekend with his large family and his friends. He was never quite ready when share time arrived because he was still writing. His classmates were amused but expected him to continue until he was satisfied, when he joined the group in the meeting place. As he began to read, audible noises of support and expectation accompanied him to the author's chair as everyone anticipated a long retelling full of rich detail.

When Donna started teaching second grade, she thought weekend news would seem too babyish to her students. She was wrong. They looked forward to the ritual of writing about their weekend the first thing Monday morning. It provided concrete evidence of growth over time with a new edition each week to look at and compare. The writing of weekend news is one way students chart their growth as writers (discussed in Chapter 9).

To help students organize their thoughts before writing, Donna suggests they decide if their retelling of weekend events will take the shape of a mitten or a glove. A glove format means the child writes about a number of different things that happened (see Figure 7–1). Mitten-shaped news focuses on one main event and tells details about that incident (see Figure 7–2). Students easily see the difference between the two formats and decide which better suits their writing on that particular day.

Some weekends are best forgotten, such as when a child is sick in bed or had a difficult visit with a divorced parent. On these rare occasions, students may invent their weekend and write fiction. Some of their best stories have come from weekend news that never really happened.

We start weekend news time with silent writing. Five minutes is

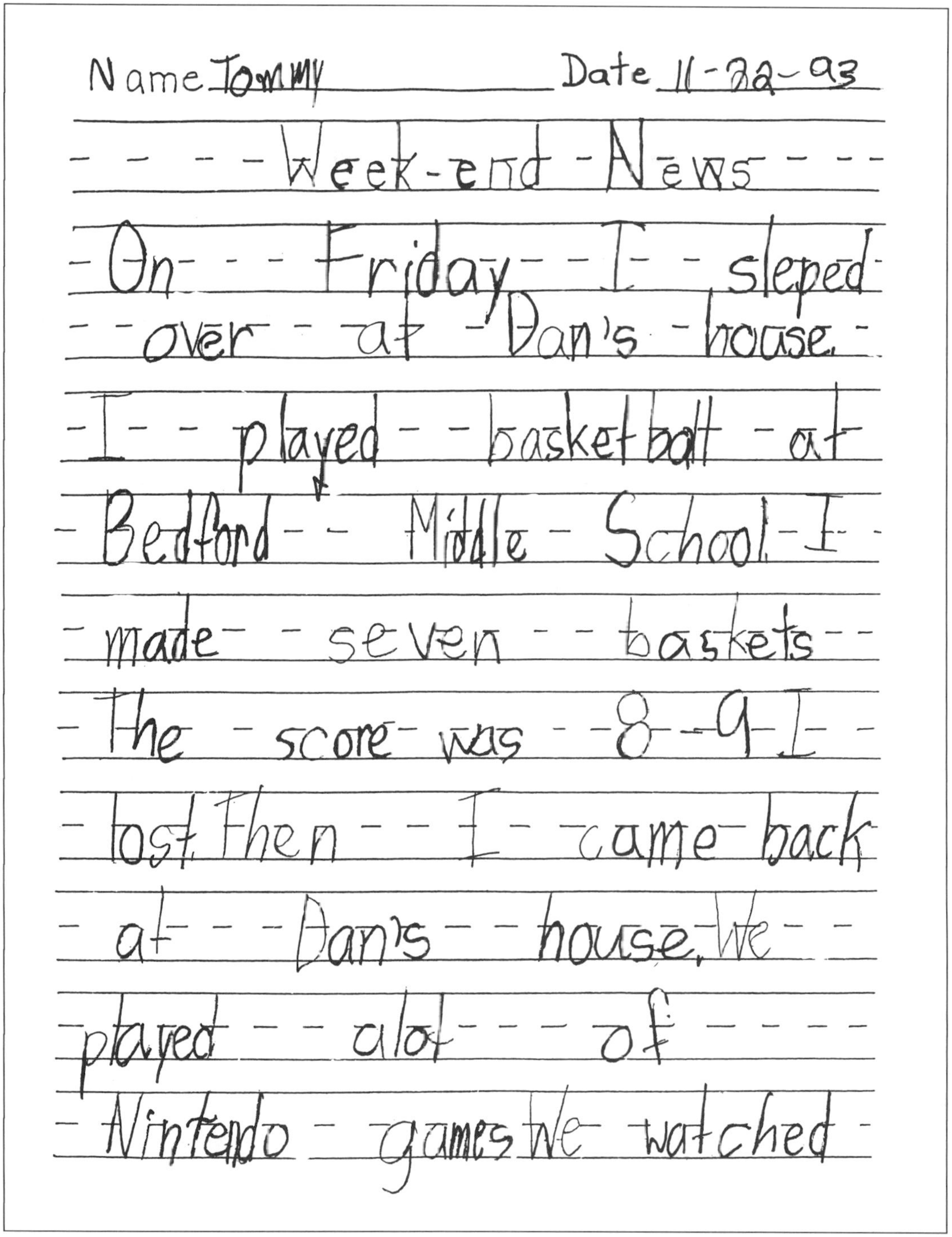

Name Tommy   Date 11-22-93

----- Week-end News ---

-On--- Friday--I--sleped-
--over--at--Dan's--house.--

-I---played---basketball--at
-Bedford---Middle--School.-I-

-made---seven---baskets--
-the--score--was--8--9 I--

-lost Then---I--came back
-at---Dan's--house. We---

-played---alot---of---
-Nintendo--games We watched-

FIGURE 7-1   First Page of Tommy's Weekend News

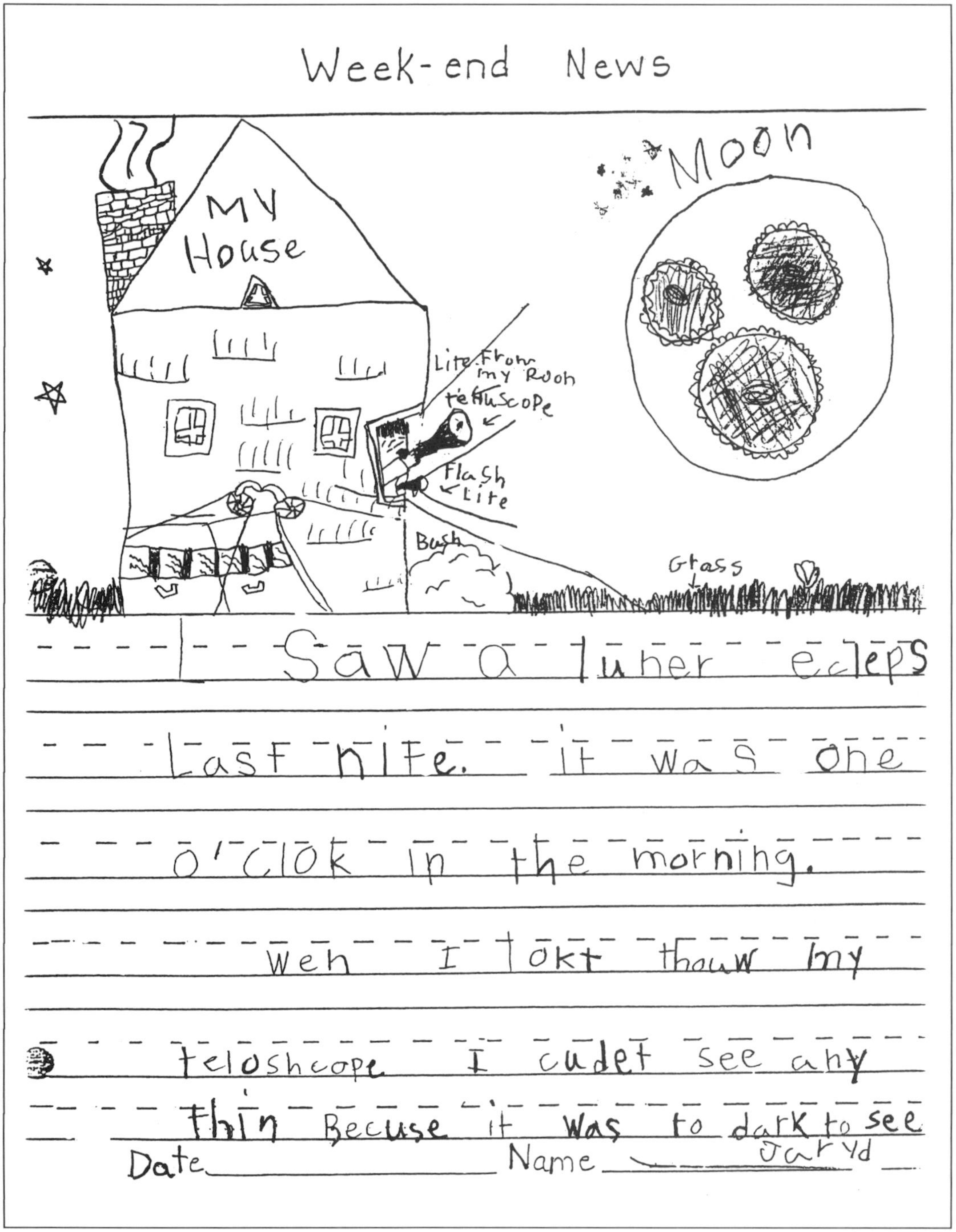

Week-end News

I Saw a luner ecleps Last nite. it was one o'clok in the morning. Weh I tokt thauw my teloshcope I cudet see any thin Becuse it was to dark to see

Date_____ Name_____ JaryD

FIGURE 7–2 Jaryd's Weekend News

enough in the beginning of the year, but this grows to fifteen or twenty minutes by June. Later, sitting in a circle on the rug and listening to what everyone—including the teacher—did over the weekend is a Monday morning ritual students anticipate. It's a relaxing way to begin the week together and helps consolidate the community after a weekend away.

Journals

As we changed our thinking about teaching and learning, we began to observe, record, and reflect upon daily events in the classroom. This journal keeping led us to realize the value of keeping a record for future reading and reflection. Just as we value our journals, so we teach our students to prize theirs as a source of discoveries about themselves and their learning.

Composition books in students' desks serve as journals for math and science. They have a special notebook for keeping personal thoughts, questions, and observations that may be the seeds for later writing pieces. Later in the year students keep journals for reader responses to novels and text sets.

All the teaching in the classroom improves journal writing. Whether we look at details, special language, or capitalization, we gradually begin to see our work reflected in the journal writing. If we are reading and discussing the craft of nonfiction, we see a carryover into journal writing. Our students begin to understand the similarities and differences in authoring fiction and nonfiction as they use journals.

Jane taught her class a solitaire game that provides practice with the addition facts for the sum of ten. After everyone learned the game and was comfortable with it, the class wrote a group story called "Tens Solitaire." This experience story helped children understand the purpose of the game as they synthesized their learning.

Next, she asked the children to record their own stories in their math journals. She told them the reader would be unfamiliar with the tens solitaire game and would need a careful explanation with details. Andrew wrote,

> Tens Solitaire is a fun game. It is fun and it helps us. We can learn that $6 + 4 = 10$. Also $7 + 3 = 10$. I knew those facts already but I like practicing You put a mystery card down. You don't look at it. When the game is over you can figure out what the mystery card is before you see it.

Science journals help students learn to be close observers of detail.

We encourage detail in drawing and writing. During a nature walk to look at tracks in the snow, children recorded their observations in their journals. Upon returning to the room, a discussion of observations allowed students to pool their thoughts until they were ready to write journal entries. The final step was to share and add any information they learned during the share that they felt should be part of the entry.

We like Toby Fulwiler's idea (1985) of how to help children learn to think about a problem: Before we discuss a problem or question, such as rules for the class, we ask students to write their ideas in a personal notebook. Once this is done, we talk together. Writing first requires each student to give thought to the problem. Otherwise, the group discussion allows some members to coast and let the more verbal classmates do the work.

The Message Board, Pet Board, and Class Secretary

We look for opportunities to encourage writing. A message board in the room legitimizes sending a note to a friend. When Courtney was in Jane's class and her sister in Caltha Crowe's room, they passed messages to each other via our message boards.

Another means of encouraging writing is a pet board, which is a favored spot for pictures and notes about pets. A class pet can provide the impetus for messages to classmates about observations, rules, animal care, or other ideas about our animal resident.

Being the class secretary is a weekly job that also requires writing. The class secretary writes notes to other teachers with requests, thanks visitors, and does any other message writing we can delegate to students.

Amanda learned she could use writing to take a stand on issues important to her. She brought her baseball bat to school, expecting to take it outside to recess. When she was told that school rules would prevent her from doing so, she couldn't believe it. She didn't understand the safety considerations involved. She decided to write a letter to our principal, Dan Sullivan, questioning the request that the bat be left in the classroom. Jane was amazed that Amanda, a quiet child, had the nerve and the self-confidence to write the letter, which was followed by a private conference with the principal. When children do not understand the purpose of rules, it can be helpful for someone to explain the reasons—a person other than their teacher.

When Donna returned to teaching second grade after being a writing teacher for five years in the classrooms of other instructors, she found some of her assumptions challenged. Her neat and tidy notions of running a writing workshop sagged under the daily strain of real children with real personalities and real problems. Her habits as a writer served as her compass when the busy workshop time took on a life of its own. One journal entry from that first fall reads,

> The kids love writing time. Their development ranges from writing chapter books to drawing maze books. When I am in their midst, I respect their efforts and am delighted with their work. But then on the drive home I start to worry: They should be doing more publishing. They should be writing longer stories. They should all be writing with words by now.
>
> I've created a list of *shoulds* based on my experience in other classrooms. I begin the next writing workshop determined to have more rigor, more productivity, more publishing. But as I conferred with students, they guide me back on track.
>
> • Jonathan's maze book was the most important activity he did all day. His intricate designs earned him a stature and respect he needed.
>
> • Jessie loved to talk about stories with Michelle and then copy what Michelle wrote. She was still learning the sounds of letters and learning to read through her writing.
>
> • Justin's elaborate drawings of Megaman were necessary before he could tell the story.

Our writing workshops have evolved and the *shoulds* in our heads push us to examine what we are doing and why. Time and again we have found the courage to make fresh tracks in the snow as we talk with students and trust their thinking. Even in the healthiest of school cultures, there is a strong pull toward conformity. The voices of the students are the best guide for resisting our own former orthodoxies that no longer support young writers.

Writing is the most personal activity students do during the school day. It taps into who they are and how they view the world. Experienced writing teachers learn a lot about students from the stories they choose to write. We recognize the sensitivity of young writers as they expose themselves on paper.

Frankie was an intense second grader who spent the year writing episodes of his book *The Adventures of Little Red Fox*. In the final chapter, added in the spring, the little red fox wishes on birthday candles and his parents magically appear in the doorway. Did Frankie, who had lived with his grandmother since his parents' divorce, realize that he was writing his autobiography with a revised script? In the role of observer, he had reshaped events to meet his own needs in order to repair his fragmented world. With such weighty issues in some of the seemingly simple stories our students write, we strive to treat every writing effort with respect.

Before the writing workshop program began, Donna helped a fourth-grade teacher to edit student writing. Children met with her to decide on revisions to make. It was easy for her to be brilliant with someone else's writing, suggesting new leads, moving sentences around, and trying to achieve the ideal text. The following fall, after a two-week summer course with Nancie Atwell and Mary Ellen Giacobbe, Donna asked some fifth graders to write: "I am a writer" or "I am not a writer" and explain their thinking. One student wrote, "I am not a writer. My teacher changes everything I write." Another student wrote, "I am not a writer. I am a finisher. I write the assignment just to get it done." These honest words moved off the page and into her memory. Writers of all ages are fragile beings. We don't want our words to cast a long shadow over their positive attitudes and efforts. We help them as best we can, but we try never to forget that we want these students to be confident and capable writers for life.

We again find that perfect words have been written by Wallace Stegner, one of our mentors: "Every book that anyone sets out on is a voyage of discovery that may discover nothing. Any voyager may be lost at sea, like John Cabot. Nobody can teach the geography of the undiscovered. All he can do is encourage the will to explore, plus impress upon the inexperienced a few of the dos and don'ts of voyaging" (1988, 9).

Writing has a broader definition than a time to write. It is a time when all the language modes are used and strengthened. But improved language facility is not the only outcome. Children interact with each other, get to know each other better through their writing, and develop a sense of cooperation and community that impacts their lives together. Writing exposes teachers and children for what they truly are—creative, imaginative, and unique human beings.

References

Fulwiler, Toby. 1985. "Writing and Learning, Grade Three." *Language Arts* 62 (1).

Goffstein, M. B. 1984. *A Writer*. New York: Harper & Row.
Nixon, Joan Lowery. 1988. *If You Were a Writer*. New York: Four Winds Press.
Stegner, Wallace. 1988. *On the Teaching of Creative Writing: Responses to a Series of Questions*. Edited by Edward Connery Lathem. Hanover, NH: University Press of New England.

The Power Tools: Listening and Talk

8

🐑 Talk has assumed a new stature in the classroom. Educators have discovered the impact of the social group upon learning and the importance of constructing knowledge within the learning community. Talk has moved from not allowing Mary's little lamb in school to welcoming the lamb as a classroom resident. There should be a sign over the classroom door that reads, "Warning: Not speaking and participating in classroom activities is harmful to your learning growth and development."

Classroom talk takes a variety of forms. There's the informal chatter when children first enter the room in the morning and want to bring each other up to date on overnight events. There are the quiet conversations about movies, Nintendo, friendships, or sports that accompany nondemanding tasks. There are the small group conversations for problem solving in curriculum areas. There are the whole class conversations about noninstructional topics. And there are the whole class discussions that support and extend the horizons of learners.

As we wrote the chapters on reading and writing, we realized how often we call the class together to process learning. We share books, student writing, and ideas about books or stories. We talk about responses to stories, brainstorm ideas, and discuss our learning processes and our thinking. We consider social problems that arise in the group. Our strong belief in building a sense of belonging and community in the classroom underlies these times when students hear each others' voices.

Why We Talk

Talk is a powerful intellectual tool. In *Whole Language: Getting Started . . . Moving Forward,* Crafton asks, "Who does the most talking in your classroom? It's probably a good index of who is doing the most thinking" (1991, 12). Researchers have taught us a new appreciation for talk and its seminal role in learning: "We need to interpret, to shape, to represent experience. . . . One way of representing, interpreting, and shaping experience is by talking about it" (Britton 1982, 100).

Talk builds a sense of community. During an interview on National Public Radio, Fred Rogers said, "They long to belong. Many children don't know what they belong to." Talk in our classrooms links student to student and student to group. The sense of belonging rises and falls on "the sea of talk on which all our school work should be floated" (Britton, 110).

Jane's journal notes the change in her practices when she returned to the classroom.

> This year is different. I am learning to let the children do more talking and I am doing more listening. As I pull out they seem to listen better to each other. They learn from each other—I wonder if they learn more from peers than from teachers? There isn't any way I know of testing that idea unless there were a full-time teacher-researcher in the room. And even then I don't know how it could be determined. But the power of the group, of the words of seven-year-old learners, seems palpable.

Problems in the classroom may be smoothed out by class discussions. Children want to be part of making the decisions that affect their school lives and we are eager to share the responsibility for establishing rules and regulations. When kickball at recess loses its fun because of all the disputes, an organized class meeting helps to resolve the conflict.

Sharing markers caused a disturbance one day. As students took turns voicing their points of view, it was obvious that minds were changing. When we took a vote, we actually reached a consensus. The large sign at the back of Donna's room states the sharing policy. It is referred to often and, because it was a group decision, compliance seems easier. It says,

Rules for Sharing

1. The owner decides whether or not to share.
2. The owner says no with kindness.
3. When told no, we accept it politely.

Next year's class may decide that if you share with one person, you must share with all. Whatever rules they negotiate, because they talked it through and heard opinions and reasons, our sense of group has been and will be strengthened. As Jane's journal entry notes,

> Allowing the kids to talk without teacher editorials and interruptions is fascinating and telling. They seem excited and they feel so in charge. The group is coming together.

Talk sheds light on the inner concerns of our students. When the bell rings in the morning, we are ready to be the shock absorber as we listen to the personal issues in our students' lives and respond in a way that is authentic and reassuring. As students tell us of the fight between their parents or of the grandparent in the hospital or of the big win in Little League, our patient listening amid the morning's first rush of activity and our response to their stories provides a ballast to set their ship aright.

Talk serves the intellectual growth of our students as well as their social and emotional needs. It invites us into their lives and gives us a gauge on their thinking. We learn from listening to our students in both formal and informal conversation. It helps us determine their self-confidence, their experiences, their strategies for learning, and their knowledge base. It gives us a glimpse into how they view the world.

SPENCER (speculatively): When you die you go to heaven and then you get another life. You get to be a baby again.
KEVIN (the practical and literal seven-year-old): How do you know? Have you ever seen it happen?

As we listen to a child our purpose is to discover the person behind the words. When Sophie says, "I don't get this," like many other statements children make, it is a multiple-choice test for the teacher. Does Sophie mean

a. help me to understand,
b. I don't know how and I don't want to know,
c. I didn't get this right away so I want to give up,
d. I'm not smart enough to learn this, or
e. all of the above?

The more sensitive we are to the signals and meanings of our students, the more on target our responses can be and the better we are able to assist them in their learning.

Jane's class discussed *Little House in the Big Woods* (Wilder 1953) after she finished reading it aloud. The discussion helped assess what had been learned from the story and what misunderstandings needed to be cleared up.

VANESSA: I liked how the father told stories to Laura and Mary. He
    was creative and had a good imagination.
MICHAEL: I learned how to make bullets.
COURTNEY: I learned how to make cheese and how to take corn off
    the cob.
KATHERINE: It leaves you in suspense. You don't know what is going
    to happen next and you can make predictions.
SEAN: I like colonial times but they couldn't have as much fun as we
    do on Sunday.

The group needed to discuss the time period of this novel. Sean had
not realized when Laura Ingalls Wilder lived because the stories in the
book were similar to ones that might have been told of colonial times.

    In June a first-grade class visited Donna's class to hear about
second grade and ask questions about the year ahead. Jennifer Salerno,
their first-grade teacher, commented on how articulate and confident
the second-grade students were. "Your students explained everything
so clearly," she said. Donna knew her students had had many opportunities to explain their thinking and ideas. Speaking to the group was part
of the daily fare. Their ability to express themselves would serve them
well in the years to come.

How Listening and Talk Are Structured

We are the models for talking and listening. We take time, make eye
contact, give encouragement, and ask pertinent and concise follow-up
questions. We give the message to do as we do.

    Ongoing rules for talk are developed in the group and are written
on a reference chart for the wall:

How to Be a Good Group Participant

• Listen to other people.
• Say something that no one else has said.
• Piggyback on someone else's ideas if possible.
• Try to extend the ideas of someone else.
• Try to remember the question.
• Say your ideas in a few sentences.
• You may pass when it is your turn.
• Use good body language including eye contact.

Jane observes in her journal that

> The listening has improved, like going over a bumpy gravel
> road which suddenly becomes paved. Even Jana, with her
> serious hearing problems, seems to hear her classmates more

easily than she hears adults. She doesn't need the Phonic Ear. Today Jamal pointed to the patterns he saw in the song on our chart [The Green Speckled Frogs]. Later in the morning Jana proudly showed me the patterns she was putting in her piece of writing.

If the listening or the sharing skills of our students need to be honed during the year, we have a minilesson before the talk begins. The focus may be any of the following:

• Why is it important to be a good listener?
• Review the reference chart "Being a Good Listener."
• What did you learn in readers' share yesterday?
• Discuss what you learned after this share today.
• How do I know when someone is listening to me?
• Role-play a talk situation.
• Why do we have readers'/writers' share?
• Should you share an idea if you're not certain about it?
• Is it good to try out an idea in the group?
• Is it OK to take someone else's idea and use it in your writing?

We model a variety of strategies about how to talk and listen in our share sessions. Over time the responsibility for what will be said becomes theirs. As students refer to the chart focusing on what they can write about a book, they realize that the list is the same for an oral or a written share.

Individuals and book groups are expected to come to a class share session prepared for talk. We encourage planning. If students are reading individual books, they have thought about their responses as they have written them. If they are working with others, they have already tested their ideas in the group of children reading together.

In *When Writers Read,* Jane Hansen says of reading talk that "when we give them the responsibility of response, they know they must generate comments and questions; we teach them to build upon each other's contributions, rather than permitting each child to offer his or her own idiosyncratic response . . . the notions they discuss will provoke more thinking" (1987, 84).

While patterns for readers' or writers' shares are established from the beginning, we add to our expectations as the year progresses. We try to be consistent from child to child and from day to day. At the same time we work to avoid the solidly ingrained pattern that becomes deadly if it is repeated day after day and week after week.

Tom Newkirk says that "the share groups that failed were the ones that lacked social interaction and energy; they stuck to questions and answers (usually formulaic) about the book. They seemed to lack digressionary possibility. They never moved" (1992, 93). We may take a passive role when it seems as if our students are off topic. They learn to take the responsibility of getting themselves back on the track. Our experiences have taught us that digressions are often fruitful.

The discussion about *Now One Foot, Now the Other* (de Paola 1980) evolved to sharing about sick relatives. It seemed off task. Suddenly Michael, the self-appointed class judge, said, "I think we should get back to talking about our book." The discussion took on a new energy. The children became extremely interested in whether a young person could actually help an ill grandparent as Tomie de Paola described.

Readers and Writers Talk and Listen

Reading and writing conversations help us measure what children are learning and thinking. We record the talk in our journals for later reflection and planning and to help us decide what needs to be done in the classroom tomorrow and next month. At the beginning of the year Jane asked her students what they were hoping to do better as readers.

RACHEL: Understand more words.
BRIAN: Do better by reading, reading, reading, reading.
NATHAN: Learn to read a little faster.
MICHAEL: I'm interested in nonfiction.
ALLISON: Read longer books.

Their responses confirmed what she suspected about where to begin. Simply reading words was not to be the goal in this classroom. We induct our students into the club—teach about reader response and reading/writing connections. As the year progressed, students used critical thinking as they shared their ideas, which is reflected in this share conducted after reading fairy tales.

NATHAN: I like this version of *Little Red Riding Hood* [Hyman 1983]. [*He reads from the book.*] The style is different from the one James Marshall illustrated [Karlin 1989]. It is more serious. The pictures are, too.
CHRIS: I like the repeating language the author used [Galdone 1984].
KATHERINE: This story reminds me of Henny Penny [Martin 1985].
PAUL: It seems like in fairy tales the older sister is always mean [San Souci 1989]. [His comment provoked a hot and heavy discussion about whether or not this was true. Examples of mean sisters

from *Mufaro's Beautiful Daughters* (Steptoe 1987) and *Cinderella* were cited.]

In time, students become adept at good conversations and there is more interaction. Discussions begin to have purpose, listening is attentive, and responses are on target.

RACHEL: I think Sarah Ida's parents probably really love her [Bulla 1975]. They sent her to Florida because they wanted to help her.

COURTNEY: Rachel, I agree with you, but what if Sarah Ida's parents won't let her come home? What if they plan to have her stay with Aunt Claudia and go to school in Florida but haven't told her?

NATHAN: It's possible that Sarah Ida will change her mind and want to stay with Aunt Claudia because she likes it now because she is working with Al. What do you think?

As Jane writes in her journal:

> I'm glad I asked the kids if they liked reading *Stay Away from Simon* [Carrick 1985] together. I don't know if I ever asked a question like that before. Imagine asking for student input. Opinions varied. Rob said he did, he got writing ideas. Randy said he liked talking together because he got help with his responses. Latisha said she didn't like it; she liked doing her own response sheets better. Alex, Shazia, Tina, and Aaron all said they liked reading a chapter book. Aaron said he thought it was nice for everyone to share the same book. Tina said she thought about the story before she went to bed and tried to figure out what was going to happen next. It feels good to have asked. I learned a lot about what they are thinking.

The class is discussing David's piece "The Big Joke Book." Jane focuses her students on word choice. During writing shares she has often heard seven-year-olds telling each other "You *should* change the way you started the story to make it more interesting." She suggests they use the word *could* rather than *should* since the decision is really in David's hands. Students responded positively and followed the practice carefully for the balance of the year. They liked the idea that the choice belonged to the author and seemed more receptive to ideas offered this way. Another journal entry records the impact of peer comments.

> In share yesterday the group told Aaron he might add more to his piece. I never saw him even slightly interested in

making changes before. He usually likes his writing exactly the way the words fall out of his head. He actually began adding today. The group sure has an impact.

A relaxed conversation at snack break about a book that was read aloud earlier in the day indicates that students are connecting literature to their own lives:

RACHEL: Did you know that Muggie Maggie [Cleary 1990] was reading the teacher's notes in the hall?
COURTNEY: I don't think that was nice.
NATHAN: But the teacher wanted her to do that.
RACHEL: Do you *really* think so? Would you do that?

Jane smiled as she overheard this tidbit. These students were so taken by the plot of this novel that they discussed it at their table as if it were classroom gossip.

Talk That Serves the Community of Learners

The status-of-the-class talk before writing workshop is a way for students to know what their fellow writers are doing. Once the routine is established, students tend to stop listening to the replies. Asking a variety of questions keeps them in touch with the work of other writers. Questions for a quick whip might be:

1. Where did you get the idea for your piece?
2. Who is your audience?
3. What is the challenge for you in your writing today?
4. How long have you been working on today's piece?
5. Who has helped you on this piece so far?

The purpose is to shift the information from the teacher's journal to the community of writers. This shift makes the sharing useful for everyone while permitting each writer's voice to be heard before writing begins.

As we process our classroom life, we discover creative ideas that spring from conversations like waterfalls from steep mountainsides. Jane's class had made vegetable soup in September. An experience chart became a newsletter to parents.

Room 13 News
Vegetable Soup

We made vegetable soup. We got the idea from a book called *Growing Vegetable Soup,* by Lois Ehlert [1987]. We cut the vegetables. We had a cutting board. Everybody got a chance to cut vegetables.

We put in green pepper, carrots, broccoli, corn, onions, potato, zucchini, tomato, cabbage, and string beans. Water made the broth. We cooked it to make it soup.

It tasted delicious.

Rereading this in November, Hallie remarked that it sounded like a poem. Carpe diem! The group began to experiment. It doesn't take much imagination to see James Marshall's influence on the ending of this much revised poem. It read as follows:

Veggie Soup
by Room 13

Veggies
washed and cut.
Green pepper, carrots, broccoli
corn, onions, potato
zucchini, tomato
cabbage and string beans.
Covered by water
cooked to broth
vegetable soup.
Yummers!

This poem became a classroom favorite. We read and recited it often throughout the year as we remembered our delicious soup.

Readers' Theater and Drama

Readers' theater is an activity second graders enjoy. It exemplifies the strategic practice of shared decision making (see Figure 4–1). Conversations around the implementation of a readers' theater piece serve the community of learners as they make decisions about a script and practice and perform it.

Our colleague Judy Luster gave readers' theater workshops in our district and taught us how to rewrite book text as a play. Each speaker in the story is read by a different child and a narrator reads the descriptive text. We have rewritten a number of picture books as readers' theater scripts. We duplicate scripts for each speaker and highlight their parts. After hearing the book read aloud, students are enthusiastic about performing it as a play. Once the class had done *Bony-Legs* (Cole 1983), *The Ghost Eye Tree* (Martin and Archambault 1985), and *Joe on Sunday* (Blundell 1987), students began turning books they had read into plays.

Jordan and Rob laughed at the silly antics in *Gus and Buster Work Things Out* (Bronin 1975). They realized the frequent dialogue would be easy to adapt. They worked together to choose a chapter to perform and decided their parts. They invited Casey to be the narrator. The class loved watching Gus and Buster and their sibling squabbles. *Gus and Buster Work Things Out* became a book in high demand.

Children may decide to improvise a story into a play. Kristy directed a group of eight young actors in their performance of *The Wonderful Wizard of Oz* (Baum 1987). The hardest part for Kristy was assigning the parts. Once the group reached consensus on that issue, the play moved forward with less grinding of gears.

The Fox books, (Marshall 1988–93), are comfortable reading for most second graders early in the year. Donna's class decided the third week in October was "Fox Week" in room 14. Donna gathered multiple copies and gave students a sheet listing all the Fox books. The students were to read as many Fox books as they could and to color in their rating of the book on the sheet. Next they chose groups, decided on a chapter from a Fox book they wanted to do for a puppet show, and made puppets using paper bags or tongue depressors. While they read the books, Donna asked them to keep track of what made Fox funny. Before they presented their puppet shows, the class shared ideas about what made Fox a humorous and lovable character. During their performances, students accented the characteristics of Fox that always seemed to get a laugh. "Oh, rats!" and "Hot dog!" became frequent phrases in the room after Fox week.

Keeping this age group from attempting a Cecil B. DeMille production is a challenge. Very quickly they plan elaborate scenery, costumes, and props. Without timely intervention, the entire project can spin out of control. If the young thespians can limit their efforts, drama is a beneficial and entertaining way for them to make personal connections to literature.

Working on projects or productions invites students to be risk takers. Because they are not pencil-and-paper tasks, they give children with strengths in other areas the chance to shine. Christina found reading an onerous task, but she took on a proud stature and clear loud voice when she performed in plays. She voluntarily took her lines home to practice until she knew them by heart. The audience never guessed that Christina was not a fluent, accomplished reader. Her reading improved as she willingly read and reread the play.

Like project work, dramatic activities allow students to be decision makers. As they choose an activity, settle on who participates, and plan the steps to completion, children have a voice in what is important to them. Some second graders fancy themselves ready for the world. Working on projects and productions lets them try their wings as they go from fledglings to flight. Careful and almost invisible intervention can help assure success and inspire students to stretch even farther the next time.

Projects and productions also put students in situations that demand cooperation. Students must sublimate their own wants and work for the good of the group if they are to be successful members of a cast. Collaboration reaches new heights when students initiate a project, feel passionate about its success, and toil to make it perfect. Our kindly advice to a student to be more cooperative with peers seems puny next to the powerful pull of a collaborative effort that is in jeopardy. Peer pressure becomes a positive force.

Talk That Serves Critical Thinking

We want our students to be aware of their thinking and to understand the purposes of activities such as reading response share meetings.

JANE: Why do we have reading response shares?

VANESSA: Because another person may get interested in the book you're reading.

MIKE: So we can talk with someone else about that book.

JANE: Why would you want to do that?

MIKE: So we can get ideas about how to write our responses.

RACHEL: We could read the book flaps and use the information about the author to help us with our response.

Rachel sent the class in a new direction for thinking about writing responses. Many children practiced her idea in the coming days.

Returning to previous questions illustrates for children the recursive nature of learning. Later in the year when the same question was posed again, there were additional answers.

NATHAN: I understand a book better when I talk about it with someone.

DAVID: The share helps me decide what I think. I like listening to other people.

ALLISON: Sometimes I think I read too fast and I miss things. It is good to hear what other people think. It helps me understand the book.

This conversation opened up avenues for diagnosis, nudging, and extending. The children were all at different levels in their development, a fact made plainly evident by the talk.

When we ask children their opinions, we follow up with the question "Why?" After a few months, students incorporate their reason into their answer without the prompt. When Casey said he liked the illustrations by James Stevenson, he paused and then told us he liked the way the splotches of paint became pictures. Jane notes some interesting connections in her journal.

> Ashley's mom came today and did a picture person lesson on Paul Klee. These kids have really learned to talk with each other about their thinking. What I noticed the most was that they use the same strategies and ideas for talking about art as they do when they talk about books or about their writing. Phrases like "I wonder where he got that idea," "that reminds me of . . .," and "I like the details he put in the figures." It was wonderful to sit back and listen to them, notebook in hand, as they critiqued each reproduction she showed.

We use "quickie" shares to utilize what would otherwise be dead time such as the few minutes before lunch or dismissal. These may include:

• book talks by children to recommend books to their peers,
• a round of compliments to classmates for something special like a job well done or being helpful to someone, or
• a rehearsal for sharing at home something that has occurred during the school day.

The rehearsal for sharing at home is structured by a question such as, "What will you tell your parents you did during reading today?" As we go around the circle and students listen to each other, they get ideas. This is helpful for those who have not yet learned how to communicate about their day at school.

Talk That Serves the Social Group

One of the knots second graders struggle to untie is how to maintain friendships. For some children, social relationships eclipse everything. If Bridget cannot sit near or work with a friend, she feels invisible. In contrast, Ashley works contentedly alone. Jane notes in her journal that children recognize the help a writer can receive from a peer conference.

> Kate told the class she got help for her story from Ebony. She said Ebony helped her think about what they did together and it made it easier for her to write her piece "The Beach."

The social interactions in the classroom may become paramount. How children talk with each other sets the tone for the day.

After Jane read *The Good Guy Club* (Dillon 1980) to the class, students decided they needed a Good Guy Club in the room. A lengthy meeting took place in which children talked about their sensitive issues and what hurt their feelings. The class drafted this statement:

> I will try not to say hurtful things about other kids.
> I will not tease others about their names, size, appearance,
>   family, staying back, or friends.
> I will not tell secrets.
>   Signed by: ＿＿＿＿＿＿

Only children who promised to make the commitment signed the large chart paper. All names gradually appeared. Bryan wrote his with a *maybe* next to it, showing Jane that he knew saying hurtful things was still a problem for him.

Miguel, a special-needs student, suggested we discuss why the children were so afraid of Simon in *Stay Away from Simon* (Carrick 1985). This question was closely related to his own problems in the peer group. In the following discussion, Miguel was able to state how Simon may have felt, which was helpful to him in establishing better relationships in the class.

A weekly class meeting helps the group resolve knotty social issues and problems of group living that inevitably arise. Students generally suggest the items for discussion and put them in a suggestion box. We sit in a circle and begin with compliments for each other. Then, after the issue is stated, everyone who wishes makes a suggestion for a solution. An agreement or some type of consensus ends the meeting. Jane's journal recalls a narrow escape.

> Class meeting relieves me from taking the sole responsibility for making decisions and puts some of it on the group. Today we talked about what to do with litter in the room after snack. Suggestions varied. Some still placed me in the central role. I could have a paper and write down the names of the offenders. When someone had their name on the paper ten times they would have to clean up the entire room. What a nightmare. Thank goodness the group decided to adopt Jen's idea. Each table would have a box to collect litter and one person would be responsible for dumping it, taking turns. We'll see how long it works.

Talking about issues and concerns takes time from academic pursuits, but it is necessary to clear the air and create an atmosphere of caring and safety. Students are more ready to dive into a learning task when they feel understood and supported by those working elbow to elbow with them.

Words are power tools. They can reassure and build. They can hurt and destroy. We try to help our students realize that the words they choose, both orally and in writing, make a difference. Even second graders understand Mark Twain's view that the importance of the right word is the difference between lightning and lightning bug. We also recognize the power of our words made weighty by our adult status. We tell Sophie she looks great in purple and Alex that he was patient with Brent. We celebrate accomplishments and encourage risk taking. We are deliberate in our choice of words, for we know they may echo back for the child long after we have forgotten them. In *Life in a Crowded Place,* Peterson writes, "Learning . . . requires practice informed by knowledgeable criticism. Opportunity to work at what is to be learned, coupled with feedback from someone who knows the territory, facilitates learning" (1992, 79).

Talking together lets students stand on each other's shoulders as they become joint creators of meaning. When partners work on a response and share ideas, the response is enhanced. When students talk together or with teachers, meaning is refined and improved.

We remember the days when most of the talking in the classroom was done by adults. Now we take pleasure in stepping back and listening as our students help us to shape the days and our teaching. Unlike childhood in the past when silence was considered to be golden, the quiet buzz of work and thinking informs our second-grade classrooms. The talk is both formal and informal and occurs throughout the day. We validate and honor it.

As Katherine Paterson writes in *The Spying Heart,* "Children tend not to say what we want to hear when we want to hear it, but to the patient, perceptive adult who takes them seriously, their words are eloquent, disturbing, and transforming" (1988, 88). There are many layers to talk in the room, just as there are many layers in fine literature. Surface layers intrude upon the day—school announcements, the day's schedule, and necessary information for all to know. Thoughtful group conversations reach below the surface and require more of the participants. Some talk dives deeper into the private realms of the child who has the courage to reveal. It all becomes part of the great mosaic of stories that fill our rooms and coalesce our lives.

References

Baum, L. Frank. 1987. *The Wonderful Wizard of Oz.* New York: William Morrow.

Blundell, Tony. 1987. *Joe on Sunday.* New York: Dial Books for Young Readers.

Britton, James. 1982. *Prospect and Retrospect: Selected Essays of James Britton*. Edited by Gordon M. Pradl. Portsmouth, NH: Boynton/Cook.

Bronin, Andrew. 1975. *Gus and Buster Work Things Out*. New York: Coward.

Bulla, Clyde. 1975. *Shoeshine Girl*. New York: The Trumpet Club.

Carrick, Carol. 1985. *Stay Away from Simon*. New York: Clarion Books.

Cleary, Beverly. 1990. *Muggie Maggie*. New York: Morrow Junior Books.

Cole, Joanna. 1983. *Bony-Legs*. New York: Four Winds Press.

Crafton, Linda K. 1991. *Whole Language: Getting Started . . . Moving Forward*. Katonah, NY: Richard C. Owen.

de Paola, Tomie. 1980. *Now One Foot, Now the Other*. New York: Putnam.

Dillon, Barbara. 1980 *The Good Guy Club*. New York: Bantam Books.

Ehlert, Lois. 1987. *Growing Vegetable Soup*. San Diego, CA: Harcourt, Brace, Jovanovich.

Galdone, Paul. 1984. *Teeny, Tiny Woman: A Ghost Story*. New York: Clarion Books.

Hansen, Jane. 1987. *When Writers Read*. Portsmouth, NH: Heinemann.

Hyman, Trina Schart. 1983. *Little Red Riding Hood*. New York: Holiday House.

Karlin, Barbara. 1989. *Cinderella*. Boston: Little, Brown.

Marshall, James. 1988–93. *Fox series*. New York: Dial.

Martin, Bill Jr., and John Archambault. 1985. *The Ghost Eye Tree*. New York: Holt, Rinehart and Winston.

Martin, Rafe. 1985. *Foolish Rabbit's Big Mistake*. New York: Putnam.

Newkirk, Tom. 1992. *Listening In*. Portsmouth, NH: Heinemann.

Paterson, Katherine. 1988. *The Spying Heart: More Thoughts on Reading and Writing Books for Children*. New York: Lodestar.

Peterson, Ralph. 1992. *Life in a Crowded Place*. Portsmouth, NH: Heinemann.

San Souci, Robert D. 1989. *The Talking Eggs*. New York: Dial Books for Young Readers.

Steptoe, John. 1987. *Mufaro's Beautiful Daughters*. New York: Lothrop, Lee & Shepard.

Wilder, Laura Ingalls. 1953. *Little House in the Big Woods*. New York: Harper & Row.

Reflection and Evaluation 9

The evaluator in the classroom holds the power. If that power resides solely with the teacher, it is within the teacher's domain to decide the success and failure of each student. As we look closely at the role of evaluation, we realize that how we judge our students has a serious impact upon how they feel about themselves. We have the power to make children

- active or passive,
- thoughtful or superficial,
- reflective or nonreflective,
- enlarged or diminished,
- meaning makers or receivers,
- independent or dependent, and
- question marks or periods.

Self-evaluation allows students to take on the characteristics on the left side of the above list. Embedded in self-evaluation are the questions, What do I think and why? For students to be full practitioners in their own learning, they have to be active participants in their own evaluation. We all have a built-in monitoring system. We want our students to fine-tune theirs as they draw conclusions about their own work and behavior. Judging their own performance forces students to think about what they have done and to decide its merits. Self-evaluation can become the easy companion of the growing literacy skills of second graders.

We look at students and try to help the individuals reach their potential. Each child starts from an individual place with a different background and set of experiences. We understand that as we teach the class to self-monitor behavior and performance, every person will take the specific strategies we discuss and use them in a unique way.

Early in life Tom learned to follow his own interests with enthusiasm. He does what he wants to do, sometimes without regard for others. Stephanie, on the other hand, is dependent, looking to other children and adults for guidance on almost every move. She reads body language and carefully interprets words before she begins to pursue an activity in which she earnestly hopes to please. Tom sets his own priorities, Stephanie lets others set hers. Tom creates options for himself, Stephanie follows others. Tom assumes responsibility for his actions, Stephanie does not. We can help Stephanie learn to be more responsible and take initiative as we encourage her to be more self-reliant. Tom can learn to be more thoughtful of others and not to be so hard on himself when he doesn't live up to his own high expectations.

Our experiences as reading and writing teachers taught us some of the developmental limitations of second graders as evaluators. For example, second graders are impressed with length in the stories they write or in the books they read. The longest story or book must be best. Their favorite story will probably be about a subject they love. A seven-year-old will like a soccer story best if that is a personal passion. But accepting these givens, we believe second graders can and should be a part of the evaluation process. We know that with our teaching and modeling and their growing sophistication, they become better critics of their own work. Stephen Covey wrote, "It is much more ennobling to the human spirit to let people judge themselves than to judge them. And in a high trust culture, it's much more accurate" (1990, 224).

This chapter explains how we build self-evaluation and reflection into daily activities and the ways we keep track of student progress, such as portfolios and videotapes. We have created our evaluation techniques in response to our programs and our students. To have changed our ways of teaching and looking at children without changing our ways of evaluating learning would have produced a debilitating mismatch, like a bear in a desert.

One-to-Four Rating Scale
We introduce the concept of self-evaluation the first day of school. When the children have finished work on an assignment, perhaps a reading response sheet, we take two minutes to ask them to rate themselves informally using their fingers to show the score they deserve.

Like the Connecticut State Mastery Test writing sample, we use the numbers one to four, with four as the highest and most desirable score. This rating has no middle or no easy number to choose, such as three on a scale of one to five. A four-level scale forces the rater to be on one side or the other. With very little explanation, students learn to use the one to four rating scale easily and honestly.

When the students have finished working on their assignment, Jane asks, "How many of you worked very hard, stayed on task, and feel that you have earned a four?" Most hands will go up; this early in the school year almost everyone is on their best behavior. "Terrific," Jane says. "It feels good to work hard. Raise your hand if you worked hard, but maybe you were nervous or thinking about vacation still, so it wasn't your very best effort. Rate yourself a three." A few hands will go up, indicating children who are probably hard on themselves. "Sometimes, when we're tired, or we're worried about something, we just can't concentrate as well. Every once in a while there will be a day when the best you can do is a two. I don't think we had anyone who would deserve a two today."

Second graders enjoy rating themselves and raising their hand to indicate their score. They are surprisingly truthful and accurate with their judgments. Explaining what behavior would equal a four, a three, a two, or a one helps students to know what behavior is expected and appreciated. It only takes about a minute at the end of an activity to ask students to think back to how hard they worked. This quick pause to take a pulse encourages children to monitor themselves as they improve both work and behavior habits. Some self-monitoring questions we may ask our students to consider are:

• Rate how hard you worked during reading this morning.
• Rate how helpful you were during cleanup.
• Rate how well you listened during the minilesson.
• Rate how well you helped others today.
• Rate how well you came to the rug.

When we introduce a new question, we briefly explain what it would mean to earn each rating, so the students are clear about the criteria for each number. Defining the criteria also forces us to think through exactly what our goals are for students and keeps us realistic about what we expect of second graders. Over time, the children internalize the criteria and respond with a raised hand as we mention each number. Internalization helps students be aware of whether or not they are performing at their peak. After a quick pause for self-evaluation, we encourage students to strive for a four next time. It is a goal that all children can attain and the one that is based on a personal best.

The quick and silent evaluations students do every day when they score themselves with their fingers are the foundation for the more cognitive task of selecting and evaluating their pieces for portfolios. We ask them to rate their effort in reading, circle the number they rate their effort on a math sheet, or rate how well they followed the rules as they returned from lunch recess. These small steps help children learn to evaluate themselves and heighten their awareness of expected behavior and effort. Sometimes we'll stop to ask students to assess performance when there is a shared sense that everyone did a fantastic job. When all hands go into the air declaring they deserve a four, it wraps the group with warm feelings of accomplishment. Sometimes, we may ask students to take a quick survey for a different reason, as when we want to remind ourselves and the class that some diligent students were concentrating and on task. It is too easy to notice the ones who are not doing their best. Asking for an evaluation nudges students to acknowledge that their effort or behavior can and should be improved.

We make a concentrated attempt, however, not to make the children who rate themselves a two or a one feel like failures. Our requests for ratings are as neutral as possible since otherwise students would stop being honest. We try to explain the lower scores in terms of possible reasons why someone would receive them: "Perhaps you went to bed too late last night, or your brother ate the last bowl of your favorite cereal for breakfast, or you just weren't able to focus and give it your best shot today." When descriptors of the ratings are on the lighter side, it keeps students interested and accurate in their self-evaluation. The purpose of this activity is to help students monitor their own behavior, not to make someone feel like a pencil without a point.

The self-awareness prompted by the quick evaluations delivers the message that students have choices about what they do; they can follow directions, work hard, walk quietly to the rug, and feel proud of doing their best. The group norms spur children on to higher standards and better behavior.

The Weekly Rating Sheet

One way we have made self-evaluation more visual and concrete is through a weekly rating sheet. The items listed make the classroom priorities explicit (see Figure 9–1). On the first Friday afternoon, Donna passed the rating sheet out and talked with the class about what

My Evaluation of the Week:

Date: _____

Name: _____

Rating Scale: 4 Excellent
               3 Very Good
               2 O.K.
               1 Not good yet

	1	2	3	4
I helped others				
I listened to others				
I did my part to help				
My effort in reading was				
My effort in math was				
My effort in writing was				
My effort in science was				
My effort in specials was				

FIGURE 9–1 Student Weekly Rating Sheet

it would mean to get a four, a three, a two, or a one. Children were able to make suggestions about what behavior would be required for each score since the class had discussed and used the rating system informally. By coloring in the bar graph, students could see a pattern.

Filling in the graph gave children time to think back over the week. Before filling it in Donna asked them to turn to a partner to discuss the graph. The conversation was structured to include the following: "I am giving myself a three because . . ." The partner was asked to give a reaction. Talking about their scores at the tables provided them with the opportunity to find out how others scored themselves and why and gave Donna another clue to their thinking as she moved among the table groups listening to and recording their conversations in her journal.

After the rating sheets were collected, Donna realized there was a big piece of information missing: the personal thinking and reasoning behind the ratings. It would be too burdensome for second graders to write explanations for each score, so the following Friday after the class finished coloring the bar graphs, she asked each child to turn the paper over and explain one score. Christina had given herself a four in all areas but science. She wrote, "I don't like science and I didn't like my drawing of our tree. I didn't try very hard." Katharine gave herself all fours. She wrote, "I always try hard in everything." She was right. She did.

The children were beginning to establish the habit of pausing periodically and taking stock. The first few times the children filled out the graph, some were not very discriminating about their scores. A number of students were content to give themselves a four in all categories. The more mature students showed a range in their personal evaluations, an indication that the ability to self-evaluate is developmental and sharpens with practice over time.

Follow-up discussions spotlighted positive memories from the week. The class focused on why a score was selected and how to build on or improve the effort. Informal goal setting, an important habit of an active learner, evolved naturally. When children scored themselves lower or higher than Donna would have, she tried to follow the advice of Eleanor Duckworth: "The role of teaching . . . is to have the students try to explain the sense they are making, and, instead of explaining things to students, to try to understand their sense" (1987, 123).

By November, we may no longer feel the need for the weekly graph, but the class continues to discuss reflections about the past week. Children have begun to internalize the questions and are able to sit and talk without the aid of concrete graphs. Occasionally, when the class dynamic is sliding slightly off track, we may have students fill out a graph that reminds them of their responsibility to themselves and to the group.

We use a graph similar to the weekly rating sheet for reading and writing. The visual representation helps everyone appreciate the ragged progress of becoming a better reader and writer. We developed these graphs when we were townwide reading and writing teachers because students, teachers, and administrators seemed to underestimate the complexities and ambiguities of learning. It was erroneously assumed that each book that was read would be more difficult than the preceding one and that each piece of writing would be better than the one before.

Reflection on Writing

Students list the title of each piece as they finish or abandon it and color in the bar indicating their rating. The in-and-out pattern of the colored bars reminds us that writing is not smooth progressions up a stairway of skills.

As students fill in the writing record graph (see Figure 9–2), we discover valuable information for group discussions about writing. Questions include:

• How has your scoring changed over time?
• What makes one piece better than another?
• What patterns do you see in your writing?

The more we use these ratings, the more students begin self-monitoring as they work. Most often we find student ratings to be on the mark.

We call classroom life to a halt every few weeks and ask students to fill in their writing graphs, although a few highly organized students do remember to keep them up to date. Maintaining the graphs takes systematic planning and time or, like other good intentions, they would disappear in the demanding competition of things that need to be accomplished.

Evaluating Books

The reading graph asks students to list the books they read and to rate how well they liked them (see Figure 9–3). This chart is kept current during the reading period each morning. It is fun to compare graphs and share opinions about books. Ratings vary from reader to reader, with some loving most books and others demanding high standards for a book to deserve a four. This prompts many worthwhile discussions

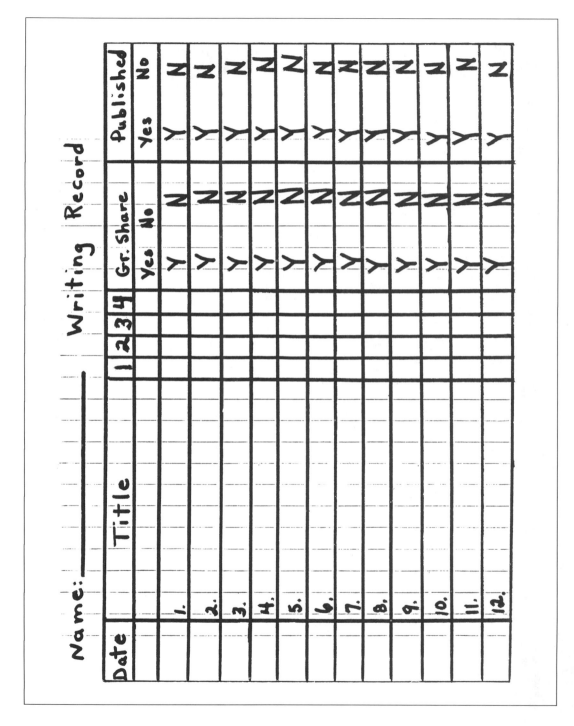

FIGURE 9–2 Student Writing Record

Date	Title	1	2	3	4

(table heading, handwritten) Reading Record & Evaluation

FIGURE 9–3 Student Reading Record and Evaluation

about what meaning the author intends and what readers bring to books.

Jane's class experienced a full variety of opinions when they finished their author study of Tomie de Paola. She gave students fourteen small squares with a title of one of his books on each square. Children stacked the squares in their order of preference, added a cover, and stapled it into a minibook. Next, students attempted to find two minibooks that matched in the order of favorites. None did. They referred to the chart "What Makes a Good Story?" but even that did not help the class reach consensus, nor was consensus the goal. The class talked about how Caldecott and Newbery award winners are chosen and what it means to evaluate books.

For math that day students used Unifix cubes to select the favorite de Paola book. They voted on how well they liked each book by dropping one to four cubes into a paper bag labeled with the book title. After they tallied the number of cubes in each bag, *Fin M'Coul: The Giant of Knockmany Hill* (1981) was declared the winner. Brendan offered to make an acceptance speech for the book and math time ended with a command performance reading of *Fin M'Coul*.

Sometimes votes for favorite books are less elaborate, but students enjoy casting their vote for the book they like best. Each Friday they vote for the book of the week. We keep track of all the books read aloud that week, and each title is listed on the chalkboard. Paper is passed out so that students can vote for their favorite. The votes are read by one student and tallied on the board by another as the tension and excitement mounts. The name of the winner is written on a piece of construction paper. The monthly lists of winners are posted in the room.

We are fascinated to discover that each class has its own personality as favorite books change from year to year and class to class. In Jane's class, chapter books are usually the winners in the week when they are finished, indicating to her that students enjoy the longer, more sustained stories that have more complex plots. This preference dovetails with the growing reading power of seven- and eight-year-olds as our students begin to read chapter books independently. They often start with a book we have read aloud as a way of feeling comfortable in this new adventure.

In June the class chooses the book of the year and time is provided to reread that book. We plan enough time before the close of school in case the book is a longer one. This rereading again models the reading strategy of revisiting a close friend. Even if we are rereading a book with suspense such as *Fantastic Mr. Fox* (Dahl 1988), students savor the reading as insiders to a secret. Rereading an acclaimed classroom favorite is a wonderful activity to spice up those last days in June.

Two years ago, Donna's class voted *The Best Christmas Pageant Ever* (Robinson 1972) as their favorite book of the year. Students enjoyed hearing again about "the worst kids in the history of the world." Donna made sure to keep the door closed during that read-aloud; she knew someone walking by in the hall would think the June stress and heat had finally overcome the teacher.

Evaluating Oneself as a Reader

Self-evaluation in reading includes two components: The first is the student effort on response sheets or reading journals, and the second is student reading habits. Stick-ems and flags add zest to self-evaluation as students look back through reading journals and put a stick-em on a page that shows their best thinking. Periodically we ask students to go back through their reading log and flag a day they remember as particularly satisfying—a day when they were lost in a book. We explore what it was that allowed the reading flow to happen. Talking about the act of reading and when it feels right gives students insights into their own reading habits and what works best for them as readers.

In January, Christopher wrote the text in Figure 9–4. He was consolidating what he had learned in kindergarten, first grade, and the first half of second grade, which included finding special language, reading book jackets, the reading/writing connection, creating reader interest by writing problems into the plot, and the patterns of several genres.

In evaluating books, response sheets, journals, and reading preferences, we ask students to think again, to reconsider their reading experiences. We ask them to grapple with who they are as readers and to make decisions about how to improve their reading habits and ability. When we ask our students to make a list in January and June of ways they've changed as readers, they are both articulate and proud of their progress.

The list from Donna's class in January helped them focus on what they had learned and included the following thoughts:

1. I can read a whole book.
2. I can read a chapter book.
3. I can read regular (not easy reader) books.
4. I read quietly.

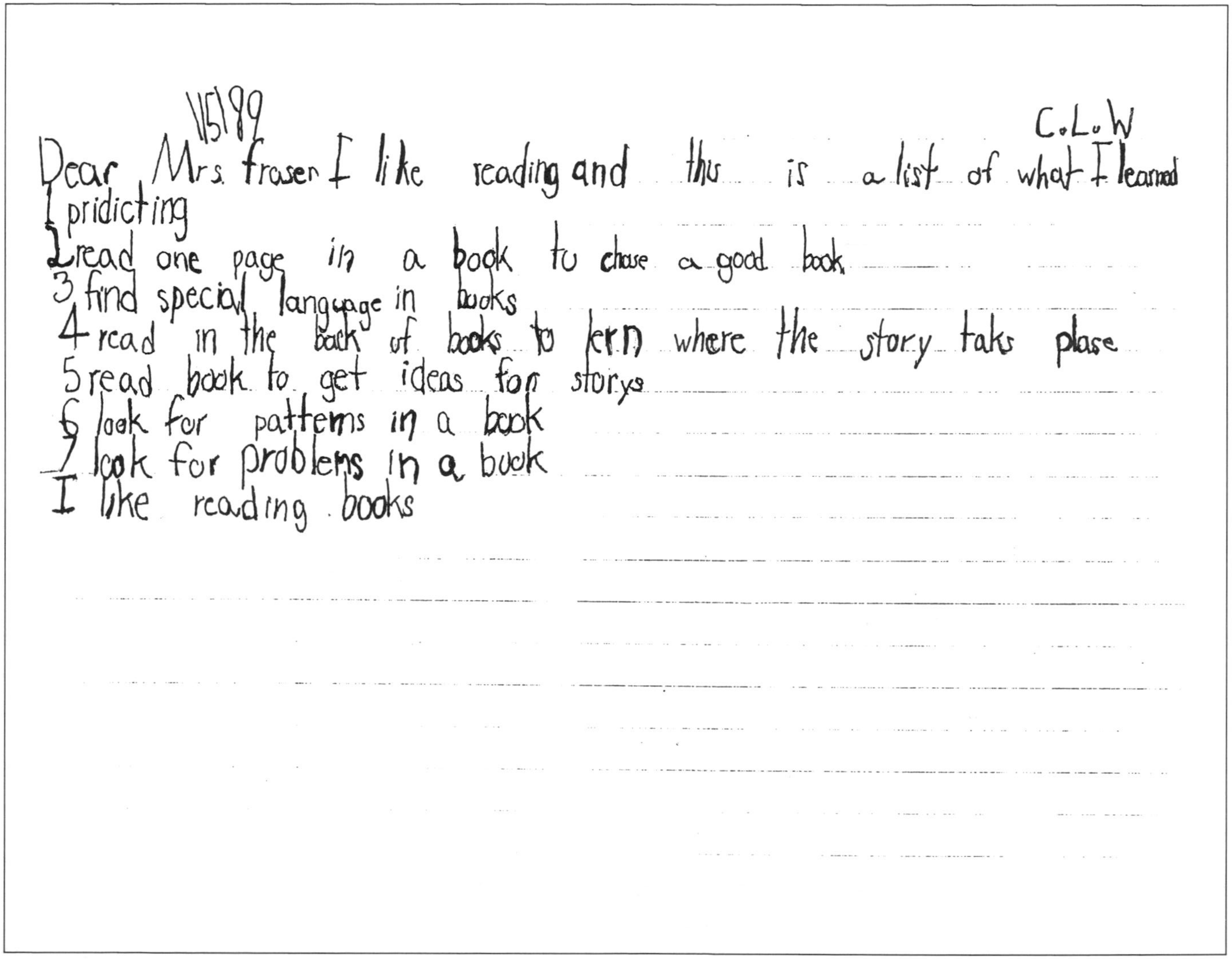

N5199

Dear Mrs. Fraser I like reading and this is a list of what I learned

1 pridicting

2 read one page in a book to chuse a god book

3 find special language in books

4 read in the back of books to lern where the story taks plase

5 read book to get ideas for storys

6 look for patterns in a book

7 look for problems in a buck

I like reading books

C.L.W

FIGURE 9–4 Chris's Self-Evaluation

5. I can read to learn things.
6. Reading is easier now.
7. I get better pictures in my head.
8. I try to predict what will happen.
9. I understand more.
10. I can enjoy books without pictures.
11. I can read more than one book at a time.

The lists vary from year to year and from January to June, but second graders report similar kinds of progress each year.

Periodic surveys or questionnaires give students time to think about their progress. The survey varies depending on the information we're seeking and the discussion we hope to generate.

In April, we wanted to highlight the reading/writing connection. The idea that our reading informed our writing was one we didn't consider until well into our adult lives. We believe our students' awareness at this young age will help them to be more critical readers and writers. The students jumped right in with ways they felt their writing was improved by their reading.

WALT: It gives me good ideas.
SCOTTIE: I notice writing signs when I'm reading and it helps me know how to use them when I'm writing. You know, writing signs like periods, quotation marks. Stuff like that.
KIRA: I'm learning to show where people are talking the way they do in books.
GABRIELLE: I learn new words that I can use when I'm writing.

Five other students wrote that they learned new and bigger words that they tried to use in their own writing.

Another question on the April survey asked students what they felt to be their biggest problem as readers. Children demonstrated insight about their stumbling blocks. Tommy answered the survey question this way, "I read too fast and then I don't understand." Students who have moved to reading chapter books seem to go through a phase when finishing the book takes priority over comprehension. As Rebecca said, "When I read too fast I can't get really good pictures in my head." But she feels a pressure to keep reading. Paul wrote, "When I rush, I sometimes skip writing signs and that makes it hard to understand." Other students felt their biggest problem was hard words. Donna knew she had to do more work on dealing with unfamiliar words in a story.

The next day's morning message carried this closing warning: "Any trading cards visible during work time will be confiscated." Since baseball and X-Men cards had recently invaded the classroom, the message grabbed student attention. The discussion about the meaning of *confiscated* stressed several strategies for finding out what an unfamiliar word means. Children quickly realized that being able to pronounce the word was only half the battle. Even if they could say *confiscate*, if it was a new word, they still wouldn't know its meaning.

The information on reading and writing surveys invites students to take a closer look at themselves as readers and writers. It also gives us information to keep our reading and writing programs closely aligned with student needs and concerns.

In his book *The Whole Story: Natural Learning and the Acquisition of Literacy in the Classroom,* Brian Cambourne writes,

> Those whom I've considered to be the most effective users of reading and writing are also those who can tell me the most about the processes and knowledge they use in order to read and write. They display high levels of what I have previously referred to as "meta-textual awareness," that is, conscious awareness of how they read and write, how they deal with reading and writing problems, how they learn, and so on. (1989, 197)

Portfolios

As we began giving our students more control of their own learning in reading and writing workshops, keeping portfolios seemed to be a logical evolutionary step. We learned about portfolios through attending numerous workshops and by reading extensively. The idea seemed a valid one. We wanted to know how using portfolios in our classrooms would help young readers and writers. We hoped to invent a portfolio system that would enhance the rigor and life in our classrooms.

We joined six other teachers in our district who also wanted to explore using portfolios, meeting once a month to exchange information. During Donna's sabbatical year, she had been part of a group of twelve teachers in Tenafly, New Jersey, who were beginning their study of portfolios. Based on their discoveries and insights and the advice of others at workshops, we began talking with our students about keeping their own portfolios.

The concept of portfolio is a simple one; living it out is complex. Our first experimental year we stopped every few weeks to have children go back through their work and select something to save. They chose from among weekend news, writing pieces, reading response sheets, and other examples of their work. They wrote a brief note about why they chose the work they did and these pages were saved in a "Special Work" folder.

For some second graders, the selection process was too undefined. We had failed to give them concrete criteria for how to rate their work. They didn't want to be reminded that only a short time before they had made many more spelling mistakes or that their handwriting was large and messy. The delight we found in seeing the obvious evidence of growth was not necessarily shared by students. Looking back seemed to them unnatural and unnecessary.

These early experiences forced us to look at precisely what it was we were asking our young students to do and to reconsider the language we used when we asked them to select portfolio or "Special Work" pieces. At this stage, we viewed portfolios as a separate curriculum. It felt like we had added another time-consuming activity to an already overloaded schedule. As we met with our colleagues townwide, we admitted that this asked a lot of teachers and we were hesitant to rush into recommending our work to others.

Fortunately, by hearing about other portfolio systems, we revised and adapted what we were asking our second graders to do and—like hiking to the top of a hill and being able to see the landscape—portfolios began to make sense. In fact, they became an exciting way to extend what our readers and writers do. We are still examining, revising, and improving, but we feel our use of portfolios is now in sync with our philosophy and practice of how children learn to be readers and writers.

Our learning process about portfolios has spanned at least five years. This is not an overnight success story. At times, we find it hard to be as patient with ourselves as we are with our students, but we try to remember that our learning has its own rhythm and timetable as well. In other words, we do not claim to always be in the top group. We trust that our own slow struggle with new ideas and change keeps us in touch with the learning struggles of our students.

Beginning the Portfolio

Accumulating a portfolio is more than shoving some papers inside a folder. We began our renewed work with portfolios on a small scale. We talked with the class about the purpose of portfolios and how they are used by artists, writers, and other professionals. A red bin, labeled "Portfolio," sits on the counter and contains large manila folders with children's names. They can save work when they wish, we can add work we feel shows a special quality, and we select work together. The portfolio system has the same idea as the title of the old Lucille Ball movie *Yours, Mine, and Ours.*

Weekend news gives children an opportunity to recall events and write about them. It helps them develop fluency and a comfort level with first-draft writing from personal experiences. It is saved each Monday and shows the most obvious growth over time. We begin our portfolio work after students have had five or six weeks of news saved in a folder. Students read back through their pieces and select the one they feel is the best so far. We encourage them to spread papers out and ask a friend for advice if the selection process is difficult. Next, students write why they chose a particular piece. A list of their ideas is compiled on the board to help everyone see the possibilities.

Several weeks earlier the class had drafted a chart stating goals for a high-quality weekend news. Several children had volunteered their papers to be used on the overhead. Jane chose two at random and made them into transparencies on the copier. As the class looked at Ashley's weekend news, they listed the qualities of her paper that made it a four. Next, they talked about Bobby's paper, focusing again on what made it high-quality work. When the chart was ready to hang on the wall, it read:

What Makes a "4" Weekend News
1. Use proper punctuation. (.!?,)
2. Use lots of good details in the text.
3. Have good details in the illustration.
4. Take my time with handwriting.
5. Tell about my weekend in an interesting way.
6. Tell a lot about what I did.
7. Use nice spacing.

The chart hangs on a closet door to guide students as they decide which of their pieces is the best effort. Because weekend news is written each week, students seem to be able to evaluate their work with more objectivity than their writing workshop pieces. Perhaps they have less invested in their first-draft writing that they do at one sitting. Most children can find evidence of improvement and change even in the first six weeks of school, with an obvious change often being the length of the text. Some students have gone from three or four sentences the first week to ten or more by the middle of October. Some are also now able to spot spelling mistakes as well as notice that capitals and periods are missing from sentences. Students derive a sense of satisfaction in finding how their writing has improved.

The reasons children give for selecting their best news still reflect the concrete thinking of seven year olds. We enjoy hearing and reading about their rationale. Here are some of the reasons the children gave this past fall:

Why This Is My Best Effort

1. I like what I did that weekend.
2. It is long.
3. It is my best handwriting.
4. It was very serious.
5. It is the one I did last.
6. I took my time.
7. I told a lot about what I did.
8. It is my best illustration.

As a second step in this portfolio selection, we ask children to write what they would like to do better on future weekend news papers. Once students have jotted down their goals, we again list the ideas on the board to allow less-able students to follow the lead of those who are more adept at the evaluation and goal-setting process. We staple this sheet to their selected weekend news and save it in their portfolio. Individual goals are copied on note cards to be used as they tackle weekend news each Monday. The list we put on the board follows:

How I Want to Improve My Weekend News

1. Do more writing.
2. Tell more details.
3. Use better handwriting.
4. Use better punctuation.
5. Have better concentration.

Expanding Portfolio Evaluation

The note cards with individual goals are taped onto writing folders. When children are ready to begin writing weekend news, we give them a quick reminder to glance at their goal and to keep it in the back of their minds as they work. At the end of each month, we pause to evaluate their success as they worked toward their goals. They look at their recent work for evidence of change. Some decide to keep the goal. Others decide they have been successful and take on a new one. We chat briefly with each writer as they decide whether or not their goal has been achieved. An easy way to gather this information is to meet with small groups while the rest of the class is writing, which allows children to hear what other goals are in progress.

Every six to eight weeks children go through the process of selecting their best effort, explaining in writing why it is best, and setting a goal for the next six weeks. This material is stapled together and put in the portfolio. We follow a similar procedure in reading and writing. Students peruse both their writing folders and their reading response journals to select a piece that they think represents their best effort. Their rationale is written and this piece is saved in the portfolio.

One day in March, Rebecca came to Donna during writing workshop, saying, "I've been reading through the stories in my writing folder and the stories I wrote a while ago don't seem good anymore. I think the one I'm doing now is good or maybe even great." Donna wanted to know what made the story she was working on better. "Oh, it has more fantasy and it's a longer story," Rebecca told her. "I think my best story so far is the fourth one I wrote. If you really look closely at it, it's kind of stupid, but it is funny." She had rated some of her stories "so-so" (a two) and some "good" (a three). Donna asked her, "What makes a story fall into each category?" "It's good if it has a lot of humor. Like one of the characters in this story is dumb. His name is Uncle Bam-Bam." Rebecca and Donna laughed at the silly name and Rebecca headed back to her desk to finish organizing her writing folder.

This brief and delightful interlude showed that Rebecca could step back and look at her past writing in an objective way. She was able to read her work "more closely" and rethink the quality of the writing. Not all students will share Rebecca's insights at this point in time, but her awareness assures us that other children will achieve this level of understanding as their experience and maturity grows. In each class there are always students who forge ahead, take the greater risks, and trample the path for other learners to follow.

Setting Standards
The charts we have drafted together become the basis for our portfolio discussions. As children select the work that shows their best thinking, their best effort, or something special they have accomplished, our

conversations probe what it is that makes a fine story or a quality reading response. We could have these discussions without saving a body of work over a period of time, but asking students to make judgements about their own work nudges them to examine their work against the explicit standards adopted by the group. Children know the standard will continue to be raised as they grow and develop greater proficiency and experience as writers and readers.

Jane's class is looking at details in writing. Michael gives permission for the class to discuss his response to *The True Story of the 3 Little Pigs* (Scieszka 1989). Michael has rated this response as a two, but the class feels it is a three or a four as they point out the details Michael used when he wrote about the humor in Scieszka's retelling and Lane Smith's illustrations.

ALISON: Michael, you used details when you wrote how the picture of the sandwich shows all the cute animals which wolves eat. Ugh!
PAUL: I like the way you wrote about how it would be too bad for a wolf to leave a ham dinner without eating it and the picture shows the pig tail and the bristles on the pig's rear end. [Laughter]
NATHAN: Mike, *Wolf's honor* are really funny words. I didn't get that until you explained it.

Students help each other build a framework for evaluation as they learn to recognize quality work. The group felt Michael was too self-critical. They tried to help him see that he had done a job that was valued by others and deserved a higher rating.

Creating the charts that spell out the expectations for work is an important activity that binds the literary community. Students voice their thoughts about what makes fine work and the contributions are enlarged and validated by the group. The charts list our expectations, which were created by the group and based on their growing knowledge of the qualities of fine literature, for all to see and attempt to attain. These goals are flexible enough to embrace the unique characteristics of each student.

The next step is just as crucial: asking children to measure their work against that class standard. Saving work in a portfolio tells the story of their sustained development from September to June. The portrait provided by the portfolio illuminates their intellectual labor. Selecting, collecting, and reflecting on their work allows them to be thoughtful historians of their own learning lives. As they compare their work to the group standard, they decide what they must do to improve, which becomes their personal goal for the next six weeks.

Student-selected goals often echo what we would have chosen for them. Philip's goal last October was to write more with his illustrations. We thought that should be his goal, too. Andrew wanted to focus more on having a beginning, middle, and satisfying ending for his stories, and he was right on target as well. Bridget wanted to challenge herself by having her characters do more talking. Adding dialogue made her future stories much more interesting.

As we have all learned with our failed New Year's resolutions, setting a goal demands a lot less than striving to achieve it. Young students need frequent reminders to reevaluate their goal along with our support and advice for how to make that goal a reality. Helping them develop the habit of setting and working toward goals is an invaluable gift we can give students. For some, it fits neatly into their working schema. For others, it is as awkward as wearing shoes on the wrong feet. But with a little extra attention and patience, our students can realize the benefits of looking and planning ahead, too.

Using portfolios involves a collaborative effort: the discussions that draft the charts, the small conversations with other students to make selection decisions, and the teacher-student conferences about the contents of a portfolio and what choices the portfolio represents. Creating portfolios with students offers continuous opportunities to talk about reading and writing and to take students' thinking about their work to a deeper, more thoughtful level. We no longer see the time we spend on portfolios as a time away from other subjects. We now see it as a time when students are gaining new understandings about being a writer and a reader.

Portfolios expand our time frame as they allow our questions to become bigger and we move from examining the process of a piece to searching for patterns through a series of pieces. Our focus moves beyond the immediate to panning back in time and forward toward possibilities that are taking shape. In a musical sense, our awareness shifts from one note to the melodic line of each student's song.

Our original interest in portfolios was based on using them as an alternative to standardized tests. Now we see them as a tool for learning—a vehicle that helps young readers and writers explore the edges of their knowledge and carry their understandings to another level of awareness. A personal portfolio confirms growth and conveys the message that each student is important. It declares individuals to be central to the daily learning process and insists that they take an active part.

Portfolio work, if done with the intent we've described, flips the learning switch from passive to active. It requires students to externalize their thoughts, contribute them to the group as they establish criteria, internalize high standards, and use those standards to set goals that strive for improvement. It is the best way to measure the small miracles that we witness every day in the reading and writing of our students.

Videotaping

At the beginning of the school year we ask our students to bring in a new or used videotape. About once a month we record each of them reading a passage from a book, their weekend news, or one of the pieces they wrote during writing workshop. The taping includes several interview questions: Why did you choose this book? What do you like best about this piece of writing? When they share the contents of their life box or perform a poem for the class, we try to have the video camera handy. We view the tapes periodically to see how each child has changed over time. We send the tape home a week before our April conference with parents so they can view it and see the progress. The tape belongs to the student at the end of second grade.

Sometimes we have had a teaching assistant who is comfortable using the video camera who can record students out in the hall. We have parent helpers come to school to assist with this job as well. More often, we have videotaped students reading while the rest of the class is having silent reading or writing. Students love to be on camera and are willing to cooperate and work quietly as they await their turn. Once the routine is in place, keeping a tape of each child is quite manageable and worth the effort. Periodically viewing the tape reminds us of how far students have come and helps us reformulate where we hope they're headed.

Modeling

Much information is available to us within the context of reading and writing workshops, large and small group discussions, reading and writing conferences, and journal entries and survey responses. We value and use that information as we plan and work with our students each day to help them to better understand themselves as learners. We let students know that we constantly monitor and evaluate ourselves by making our learning visible. When we share the notes and reflections from our journals, we guide students to set and reach their own goals. Some questions we ask ourselves are mirror images of those we ask our students:

- Did our day or our week go well?
- What will we continue to work on tomorrow? next week?
- Were today's activities appropriate for the group? for particular individuals? Should those activities be continued, modified, dropped?
- What did I learn that was new?
- What will I do next with my new learning?

Evaluation is embedded in all we do. Every time we make a choice—cereal or toast for breakfast, the black skirt or the black pants, to write weekend news on paper or in journals—each decision involves evaluation. We're all pros at it.

Students who take active roles as learners can also accept an active role in evaluation. Our work as teacher-researchers encouraged us to ask students for their thinking. Time and again, their thoughtful comments amazed us. Young students were capable of understanding their own growth and progress, especially when the criteria was delineated and discussed. Thus, we have rethought our classroom practices to include evaluation. It invites our students to take a closer look at themselves as learners and to make personal decisions about progress and goals.

As new leaves grow on the oaks and maples outside our room in May and June, we see the branching structure of the trees behind the spring green. We teach seven- and eight-year-olds the framework of evaluation that underlies scholarship as their own leaves develop in our reading and writing workshops.

References

Cambourne, Brian. 1989. *The Whole Story: Natural Learning and the Acquisition of Literacy in the Classroom.* New York: Scholastic.

Covey, Stephen R. 1990. *The Seven Habits of Highly Effective People: Restoring the Character Ethic.* New York: Simon and Schuster.

Dahl, Roald. 1988. *Fantastic Mr. Fox.* New York: Puffin Books.

de Paola, Tomie. 1981. *Fin M'Coul: The Giant of Knockmany Hill.* New York: Holiday.

Duckworth, Eleanor R. 1987. *The Having of Wonderful Ideas and Other Essays on Teaching and Learning.* New York: Teachers College Press.

Robinson, Barbara. 1972. *The Best Christmas Pageant Ever.* New York: Avon.

Scieszka, Jon. 1989. *The True Story of the 3 Little Pigs.* New York: Scholastic.

Epilogue:
Keep the Music Playing

Teachers make the best of whatever we are given and keep plugging away to do our jobs well. If our class size is twenty, thirty, or forty, we take it in stride and do the best we can. Just like gerbils, we don't require a lot of maintenance; throw us some sunflower seeds and a cardboard roll to chew and we keep running on the wheel.

There are both good and bad sides to our perseverance. On the positive side, it means that we bend over backwards to compensate for what is missing. After all, it is the children who would suffer if we don't compensate. They depend on us. If our weekly schedule has been arranged in ways that prevent our teaching time from being organized for prime effectiveness, we work within that schedule to the best of our abilities. We devote our personal time in August to the organization of our rooms for that smooth beginning on the first day of school. If something is needed and is not provided, we find a way to get it or rethink the situation. How many times have we assumed responsibility for something that should have been available through the school budget? We are, by nature, a group of givers.

But we know the downside. No one expects elementary teachers to stand up and insist on being heard. It is new for many teachers to take a position of advocacy and ask to have a voice in decisions that affect their school lives and the learning lives of their students. Some of us are learning to be advocates and to assume that our voices deserve to be heard.

When Donna's children were young, she taught reading part time in a converted locker room. Each morning as she worked with second- and third-grade children struggling to learn to read, an abandoned toilet in the corner flushed and flushed. The toilet could not be used, but water continually ran through it. For some reason, it was beyond the maintenance staff to fix or remove it. Finally, a parent who found it annoying during a parent conference complained to the principal. Magically, the toilet disappeared.

The next fall, the principal and custodian decided the small reading room would be a good place to store extra supplies of paper towels and toilet paper. The room was only used in the morning so it certainly wouldn't bother anyone to have cartons of supplies stacked around the edge from floor to ceiling. Or so they reasoned.

Donna could not believe the principal had so little understanding of what it means to create a suitable and pleasurable learning environment. When Donna refused to teach in a storage room with her group of distractible seven- and eight-year-olds, this (now former) principal said, "I've never seen you like this. Why are you so upset?"

No doubt we have all encountered times in our professional careers when our only recourse was to get upset, when we knew we had to step forward and be an advocate for what we knew was best for children. The above incident occurred over ten years ago. Fortunately, over the past decade, many educators have adjusted to the new roles teachers are assuming. If conditions are to improve in schools, we cannot patiently wait for someone else to do it. The whole language movement, with all its publicity and impact, demonstrates what teachers can do at a grassroots level. Elementary teachers no longer need to be the stepchildren to the higher levels of education. What we do makes a tremendous difference in the long-term learning of children.

We are advocates both for and within our profession. We have shared our professional passions as we served on committees that we hope will help to shape change in our district. We have contributed articles to a local newspaper column called "And Gladly Teach." When an article in the *New York Times* said that many schools were experimenting with literature in their reading programs, Donna fired off a letter explaining that a literature-based reading program in her school had been in place for over ten years, was highly successful, and certainly was *not* an experiment. Who can say if readers two weeks later were influenced by her letter to the editor, but the misinformation had to be corrected. Sometimes we can be advocates through our writing, and other times we may serve on committees or be discussion leaders at staff or PTA meetings. Our professional stance is proactive.

When we first introduced reading and writing workshops into classrooms, we urged teachers to invite administrators in to learn about workshops and to understand the theory behind the practice. One articulate teacher complained that she had enough to do to continue learning how to be a better teacher. Why should she also be expected to educate her principal? But Reality often dictates that teachers must champion their own practices. They need to help administrators keep up to speed by sharing articles, professional journals, and the work of children that speaks clearly to the appropriateness of what we do.

In fact, we teach our students as well as their parents and the general public. If we want to keep them with us as we change and improve our schools, we must help them be informed and in favor of what is going on in classrooms. The conventional wisdom that the "good old days" in school were much better is a difficult concept to replace. Sometimes it feels like it must be akin to the task of convincing people in the fifteenth century that the world was round.

Teaching is a tremendous responsibility. We as teachers have the key to unlock doors or to slam them shut. Children remember our actions and our words. They see themselves reflected in our eyes and take that image to heart. Our affirmations, our patience, and our appreciation for who they are demands an energy and strength to sustain our good humor and caring. Adults who are not familiar with second graders assume young children lead uncomplicated lives, like the Bobbsey Twins. Teachers know just the opposite is true. Their worries can feel just as weighty as those of any grown-up—and sometimes more so. Young children haven't had the experience to know how to solve many of life's problems and they are dependent on adults for much in their lives.

How do we stay able to give what we want and need to provide each long day? How do we maintain our enthusiasm and energy? How do we keep the music playing? In our lengthy professional careers, we have found small and big ways to keep ourselves up to the demanding task we face each morning.

It's closing the door when the class goes to art and playing a peaceful tape by James Galway while we attempt to get organized. It's sipping a cup of coffee before school and swapping stories for five minutes with other staff members in front of the mailboxes. It's inviting four students to eat lunch in the classroom, adding a small vase of flowers to the table, and having the time to hear about their lives. It's keeping a journal so we can monitor our ups and downs and know that bad days are followed by good. It's knowing that there is more than one solution to most problems and trusting that we have the resources to help us solve pressing and stressful issues.

Within the school context, there are several factors that make our jobs feel right. Our professional freedom permits us to keep our classrooms fresh and alive. If the school days seem to be dragging, we confer with our students and create projects or themes that up the energy. When the students are excited about their work, it is impossible not to share their eagerness. Addison grabs Jane's hand and insists, "Quick, Mrs. Fraser, come see what Walt and I made with the pattern blocks. It's just like Disney World. Can you put it on my videotape?" Tommy and Scottie initiate and draw a mural of an underwater scene. They tape it up in the hall for all to admire. Alex writes a poem about his little brother that makes the class giggle. These shared moments of pride and pleasure suffuse the room with a golden glow.

This flexibility helps us enhance learning and bring variety to the day. We choose a new path when the students indicate an interest or need. Unpaved roads bring new excitement into the class as no one is certain what will happen. The unexpected, played out among the structures and rituals already in place, provides new challenges to both children and adults. We relish these opportunities because we cannot imagine doing the same thing over and over. We listen carefully for the unusual and mull over the happenings of the day and week recorded in our journals to find hints for new directions.

Each day we get a healthy dose of surprise to help keep us lighthearted and on our toes. That surprise can be Amy's creative leap when she figures out a pattern in Mary Calhoun's delightful stories about Henry, a Siamese cat. The unexpected can be Stephanie and Kelsey, students from the previous year, stopping by with a paperback book they bought as a gift for Donna at a tag sale. Or the astonishment can be when Melissa wets her pants during a math lesson, something she's not done for years. She stares wide eyed at her two friends, who are arranging pattern blocks on their desk, and announces, "I just did the most amazing thing." Whether puddles or accomplishments, we plan on being surprised.

Small teaching moments can lead to the unexpected. A colloquial usage such as *me and my brother* (as a subject) feels like gravel inside a shoe to Jane. With some passion, apparently, she told her students that this was incorrect usage. She talked about it several times when it came up in writing or conversation. Tim was intrigued by her strong stance and, as was typical for him, decided to challenge it. He began writing "ME AND MY DAD," "ME AND WILLIAM," "ME AND MY SISTER." He drew six or seven lines under those words for further emphasis. It became a classroom joke, but Jane knows he won't forget the correct usage, perhaps for the rest of his life.

Tim's teasing always brought laughter in the group. Laughter keeps us going amid the tensions, serious issues, and things that need to be done. But a second-grade sense of humor is not necessarily funny to an adult. When we hear a "knock-knock" joke for the umteenth time, we feign surprise and act like it's the first. How could a seven-year-old know that we heard it first back in 1953? We walk that fine line between being honest in our responses and responding in ways that show we delight in their sharing humor with us. Our job shifts often. We are teachers, actors, tightrope walkers, and many other professions.

We treasure our relationships with colleagues and with the administrators who have supported and nourished us. Shared moments are crucial to our well-being. Recent research quoted by Albert Shanker in the May 2, 1993, *New York Times* confirms the value of teachers working in close collaboration: "Teachers in a professional community feel more positive about their teaching and their students are more successful than youngsters taught by noncollegial teachers." Our teaching day is better because we share it with colleagues who celebrate our successes and pass the tissues when we're down. They take the time to problem-solve with us and offer their assistance. These relationships help determine the quality of our school lives.

We work hard to keep the job we do in proper perspective. We must accept our personal limits and the limitations of our job. We cannot make the world right for all the children we have come to care about. It is important for us to pause and examine what is realistic and possible. We factor in our dreams and desires for these children. As we cast our glance ahead, we see time for them to mature and grow. Our job is not to perfect each child each year. Our job is to open doors and extend possibilities. We ask that of ourselves and our students.

More than one hundred years ago, William Ellery Channing wrote,

> The great end in education is not to stamp our minds upon our students, but to stir up their own; not to make them see with our eyes, but to look steadily and inquiringly with their own; not so much to give them definite knowledge as to inspire in them a fervent love of truth; not to force upon them an outward regularity, but to release in them inward springs of inquiry; not to bind them to fixed notions of

ours, but to prepare them to judge impartially whatever subjects may be offered for their decision. (p. 449)

Last June, when Donna talked with the student teacher assigned to her in the fall, he asked if there was anything he could do to prepare for September. "Have an enriching, wonderful summer," she told him. "Relax, read, pursue your hobbies, travel, laugh. Come back in the fall feeling marvelous about yourself and your life."

We believe that we are better teachers when our personal lives are balanced and healthy. We cannot control the fates, but we can try to find time in our busy lives to do the things that make us who we are. Whether it is reading a good book, going to the opera, working in the garden, playing the piano, or going to aerobics class or on a long walk, all these respites from the hassle of life in the 1990s replenish us. We cannot be the teachers we want to be if we're running on empty. Sometimes replenishment might mean ignoring a bulletin board in the hall that has Halloween pictures in December and taking a walk at the beach after school. It might mean going to bed before everything on our endless list is finished because we know the next day at school is the Valentine's Day party and will demand patience and energy. For us to feel our day with children is truly quality time, we must be feeling good about ourselves. We continually strive to set priorities.

High on our priority list is learning. We take classes, attend workshops, belong to professional associations, and discuss how to improve our practices with colleagues. We read professional journals and books as we search for ways to extend and improve.

It has taken us years to develop the art of teaching and we're still learning. Each day brings new lessons, new surprises, and new insights. The second graders who have shared their lives with us have left us wiser and more appreciative of their capabilities and wonders. Viewing the world through their eyes has been our good fortune. We celebrate our second graders—with their missing teeth, quirky sense of humor, and keen desire to learn.

References

Calhoun, Mary. 1984. *Hot Air Henry*. New York: Morrow Junior Books.

Channing, William E. 1875. *The Works of William Ellery Channing, D.D.* Boston: American Unitarian Association.

Shanker, Albert. 1992. "Where We Stand." *New York Times News of the Week in Review* (May 2).

Appendixes

Parent Questionnaire

The following questions are sent to parents the first week of school together with a brief general letter about classroom procedures and the schedule of specials, such as gym and music.

1. What would you like me to know about your child?

2. How does your child spend time on his/her own at home?

3. What are your goals/expectations for your child this year?

Strategies to Help Your Young Readers

1. Set aside a regular time each day to share a book.

2. Read to your child with expression and pleasure.

3. Do not insist they read aloud unless they are willing. This should be a time of togetherness and warmth, not a time of teaching or testing.

4. Choose some favorite poems to read aloud. Have your child read the poems and acquire fluency. Repeated readings can be fun and very helpful if the poems are humorous. Shel Silverstein and Jack Prelutsky are two well-loved poets.

5. Recognize that reading is still a difficult and tiring task. Be supportive and patient, appreciating the effort that it requires.

6. As you read to your child, stop periodically and talk about the pictures in your imagination. Ask your child about their mental images. Some children need more help turning words into mental pictures.

7. Keep the faith. Children have individual time-tables as they learn to be fluent readers. They cannot fast-forward that development schedule anymore than they can grow to a desired height. All children do learn to read. Hold on to that belief and pass it along to your child. They are even more anxious than you are to be a star reader.

Parent Handout

READING RESPONSE SHEET

Name: _____

Date: _____

Title: _____

Author: _____

Book Conversations

Rules for meeting together and talking about books:

1. One person tells about a book at a time.

2. Look at the person speaking.

3. Keep your book closed until it is your turn.

4. Think of something you would like to know about the book.

What each reader shares about their book:

1. Title and author

2. Why they chose the book

3. How far they are into the book

4. Main characters

5. Setting

6. Story problem

7. A favorite section (read aloud)

Questions and comments from other readers:

Author Study Record

BOOKS BY JAMES MARSHALL

Date	Title	Score			
		1	2	3	4
	Fox on Wheels				
	Fox at School				
	Fox Be Nimble				
	Fox in Love				
	Fox All Week				
	Fox on the Job				
	George and Martha				
	George and Martha Encore				
	Rats on the Roof				
	Nosey Mrs. Rat				
	Three Up a Tree				
	Three by the Sea				
	Four on the Shore				
	The Stupids				
	The Stupids Die				
	The Stupids Step Out				
	The Cut-Ups				
	Yummers!				
	Yummers Too				
	Old Mother Hubbard				
	Little Red Riding Hood				
	Cinderella				

Name: _____

Reading Questionnaire

I like to read
  alot   some   a little   zip

I think reading is
  fun   o.k.   so-so   hard

This summer I read
  a lot   some   a little   zip

I like to choose books to read —
      Yes   No

I like to listen to books
      Yes   No

This year I hope to change
    as a   reader this way:

(Used the first day of school.)

General Questionnaire

Name _____   Date _____

1.) Tell us what you like about
   second grade so far:

2) Tell us something you would like
   to change about second grade:

3.) I think I listen best
   ☐ at my desk
   ☐ on the rug in a group
   ☐ on the rug in a circle

4.) I wish we had more time for:

READING SURVEY

Name _____

Date_____

I like to be read to: yes   no

I like to read to myself: yes   no

By myself, I can read _____minutes
without getting tired.

Check the kind of books you like to read:

____books where the pictures also tell the story

____books with just a few illustrations

____books that are humorous

____books about mysteries

____books that have chapters

____books about animals

____books that are true (non-fiction)

____books that are scary

____books that I already know

____books other kids say are good

____books with just a few words on a page

____books with lots of words on a page

Another kind of book I like is _____

_____

My favorite book I've read this year is:_____

Reading Survey

Name _____

Date_____

1. The book I read today is _____

2. I like this book a lot   it's O.K.   some   yuck

3. I am good at choosing books I like.   Yes   No

4. The best book I read lately is _____

5. My favorite read aloud is _____

6. My favorite author is _____

7. My reading helps me as a writer because _____

_____

8. My biggest problem as a reader is _____

_____

9. I would like you to help me get better at _____

_____

10. Topics I would like to read and learn about this year are

_____

_____

Name_____

MY WRITING RECORD

Date	Title	Rating				Comments
		1	2	3	4	

Weekend News Evaluation

Name_____

Date_____

This Weekend News is my best effort because

_____
_____
_____
_____
_____
_____
_____
_____
_____

I want to make my Weekend News even better by

_____
_____
_____
_____
_____
_____

Publishing Tips

Take the time to do
your best work.

Use your rough draft to plan
your published book.

| Title page: |
I dedicate this book to
Title and your name in capitals,
spelled correctly

Written by   Illustrated by

| Dedication page: |
I dedicate this book to
Dedicated to

| Illustrations: |
Use crayons, markers, photos, clippings....

| About the Author: |
Write draft, edit carefully

Name_____Date_____

Writing   Evaluation

1.   What I have learned about myself as a writer so far this year:

2. How I would like to get better as a writer in the next months:

3. What I've learned about writing from the books I read:

4. One problem I have as a writer:

5. My effort as a writer so far: 4   3   2   1

6. How well I like my stories: 4   3   2   1